BAPTISTWAY ADULT BIBLE STUDY GUIDE®

Living Faith in Daily Life

ROBERT PRINCE
BOB DEFOOR
JULIE WOOD
JEFF RAINES
WESLEY SHOTWELL
DIANNE SWAIM

BAPTISTWAYPRESS®
Dallas, Texas

Living Faith in Daily Life—BaptistWay Adult Bible Study Guide®
Copyright © 2010 by BAPTISTWAY PRESS®.
All rights reserved.
Printed in the United States of America.

No part of this book may be used or reproduced in any manner whatsoever without written permission except in the case of brief quotations. For information, contact BAPTISTWAY PRESS, Baptist General Convention of Texas, 333 North Washington, Dallas, TX 75246-1798.

BAPTISTWAY PRESS® is registered in U.S. Patent and Trademark Office.

Scripture marked NIV is taken from The Holy Bible, New International Version (North American Edition), copyright © 1973, 1978, 1984 by the International Bible Society. Used by permission of Zondervan Publishing House. Unless otherwise indicated, all Scripture quotations in lessons 1–7 and 10–11 are from the New International Version.

Scripture marked NASB is taken from the 1995 update of the New American Standard Bible®, Copyright © The Lockman Foundation 1960, 1962, 1963, 1968, 1971, 1972, 1973, 1975, 1977, 1995. Used by permission. Unless otherwise indicated, all Scripture quotations in lessons 8–9 are from the New American Standard Bible.

Scripture marked NRSV is taken from the New Revised Standard Version Bible, copyright 1989, Division of Christian Education of the National Council of the Churches of Christ in the United States of America. Used by permission. All rights reserved. Unless otherwise indicated, all Scripture quotations in "Introducing Living Faith in Daily Life" and lessons 12–13 are from the New Revised Standard Version.

BAPTISTWAY PRESS® Management Team
Executive Director, Baptist General Convention of Texas: Randel Everett
Director, Education/Discipleship Center: Chris Liebrum
Director, Bible Study/Discipleship Team: Phil Miller
Publisher, BAPTISTWAY PRESS®: Ross West

Cover and Interior Design and Production: Desktop Miracles, Inc.
Printing: Data Reproductions Corporation

First edition: June 2010
ISBN–13: 978–1–934731–50–5

How to Make the Best Use of This Issue

Whether you're the teacher or a student—
1. Start early in the week before your class meets.
2. Overview the study. Review the table of contents and read the study introduction. Try to see how each lesson relates to the overall study.
3. Use your Bible to read and consider prayerfully the Scripture passages for the lesson. (You'll see that each writer has chosen a favorite translation for the lessons in this issue. You're free to use the Bible translation you prefer and compare it with the translation chosen for that unit, of course.)
4. After reading all the Scripture passages in your Bible, then read the writer's comments. The comments are intended to be an aid to your study of the Bible.
5. Read the small articles—"sidebars"—in each lesson. They are intended to provide additional, enrichment information and inspiration and to encourage thought and application.
6. Try to answer for yourself the questions included in each lesson. They're intended to encourage further thought and application, and they can also be used in the class session itself.

If you're the teacher—
A. Do all of the things just mentioned, of course. As you begin the study with your class, be sure to find a way to help your class know the date on which each lesson will be studied. You might do this in one or more of the following ways:
- In the first session of the study, briefly overview the study by identifying with your class the date on which each lesson will be studied. Lead your class to write the date in the table of contents on page 7 and on the first page of each lesson.

- Make and post a chart that indicates the date on which each lesson will be studied.
- If all of your class has e-mail, send them an e-mail with the dates the lessons will be studied.
- Provide a bookmark with the lesson dates. You may want to include information about your church and then use the bookmark as an outreach tool, too. A model for a bookmark can be downloaded from www.baptistwaypress.org on the Resources for Adults page.
- Develop a sticker with the lesson dates, and place it on the table of contents or on the back cover.

B. Get a copy of the *Teaching Guide*, a companion piece to this *Study Guide*. The *Teaching Guide* contains additional Bible comments plus two teaching plans. The teaching plans in the *Teaching Guide* are intended to provide practical, easy-to-use teaching suggestions that will work in your class.

C. After you've studied the Bible passage, the lesson comments, and other material, use the teaching suggestions in the *Teaching Guide* to help you develop your plan for leading your class in studying each lesson.

D. You may want to get the additional adult Bible study comments—*Adult Online Bible Commentary*—by Dr. Jim Denison (president, The Center for Informed Faith, and theologian-in-residence, Baptist General Convention of Texas) that are available at www.baptistwaypress.org and can be downloaded free. An additional teaching plan plus teaching resource items are also available at www.baptistwaypress.org.

E. You also may want to get the enrichment teaching help that is provided on the internet by the *Baptist Standard* at www.baptiststandard.com. (Other class participants may find this information helpful, too.) Call 214-630-4571 to begin your subscription to the printed or electronic edition of the *Baptist Standard*.

F. Enjoy leading your class in discovering the meaning of the Scripture passages and in applying these passages to their lives.

Writers of This Study Guide

Robert Prince, writer of lessons one through three, serves as senior pastor of First Baptist Church, Waynesville, North Carolina. A native of Georgia, Dr. Prince has served in pastorates in that state and in Texas. He has also served as an adjunct instructor at Southwestern and New Orleans Baptist Theological Seminaries, and at Wayland Baptist University. He earned his B.A. degree from Baylor University, and his M.Div. and Ph.D. degrees from Southwestern Baptist Theological Seminary.

Bob DeFoor of Harrodsburg, Kentucky, wrote lessons four and five. Dr. DeFoor served more than forty years as a pastor of churches in Kentucky and Georgia, serving the last twenty-eight prior to retirement as pastor of Harrodsburg Baptist Church. Both Bob and his wife Sandy are native Georgians, and they are graduates of Baylor University. Bob is a veteran writer of Sunday School lessons, and his Sunday School lessons have also been heard on radio for twenty-eight years.

Julie (Brown) Wood wrote lessons six and seven. She is a graduate of Hardin-Simmons University and Southwestern Baptist Theological Seminary. A former children's minister and worship leader, she now serves as a tutor and freelance writer. Most of all, she loves ministering with her husband, Dr. Darin Wood, pastor of Central Baptist Church in Jacksonville, Texas.

Jeff Raines, writer of lessons eight and nine, is associate pastor, First Baptist Church, Amarillo, Texas. Dr. Raines is a graduate of Baylor University, Truett Seminary, and Princeton Seminary (D.Min.). He has served as the second vice president of the Baptist General Convention of Texas (2008). He and his wife, Darcie, have one son, Mark.

Wesley Shotwell wrote lessons ten and eleven. Dr. Shotwell is pastor of Ash Creek Baptist Church, Azle, Texas. He formerly was pastor of churches in Tennessee. He is a graduate of Baylor University (B.A.), Southwestern Baptist Theological Seminary (M.Div.), and Vanderbilt Divinity School (D.Min.).

Dianne Swaim, writer of lessons twelve and thirteen, is chaplain coordinator for Arkansas Hospice, Inc., in Little Rock, Arkansas. She also does chaplaincy work for the Veterans Administration Hospital in Little Rock. She has served on church staffs in Mississippi and Arkansas as minister of single adults. She has been a keynote speaker at national single adult events and speaks for single adult and women's retreats and seminars. She is the author of *Divorce Hurts Even at Church* and has written also for *Missions Mosaic Magazine* (WMU). She is a graduate of Southwestern Baptist Theological Seminary (M.Div.).

Living Faith in Daily Life

How to Make the Best Use of This Issue		3
Writers for This Study Guide		5
Introducing Living Faith in Daily Life		9

DATE OF STUDY

LESSON 1	_____	*Knowing God in Daily Life* PSALM 139:1–12, 23–24; PROVERBS 3:5–6	13
LESSON 2	_____	*Working with Heart* EXODUS 35:30–35; PROVERBS 6:6–11; COLOSSIANS 3:23–24; 2 THESSALONIANS 3:10–13	21
LESSON 3	_____	*Saying Yes to Sabbath Rest* DEUTERONOMY 5:12–15; PSALM 127:1–2; MARK 6:30–32	31
LESSON 4	_____	*Enjoying the Life God Gives* PSALM 16:7–11; ECCLESIASTES 5:18–21; LUKE 7:31–35	39
LESSON 5	_____	*Building Community* 2 KINGS 7:3–9, 16; NEHEMIAH 2:17–18; 4:6; LUKE 10:25–37	49
LESSON 6	_____	*Welcoming (Even) the Stranger* DEUTERONOMY 10:17–19; MATTHEW 25:34–40; LUKE 14:12–14; HEBREWS 13:1–2	59
LESSON 7	_____	*Forgiving the Person Who Hurt You* MATTHEW 6:12, 14–15; 18:21–35; COLOSSIANS 3:12–14	69
LESSON 8	_____	*Setting Right Priorities in a Money-Centered World* LUKE 12:15–31; 1 TIMOTHY 6:6–10, 17–19	79

LESSON 9	_____	*Engaging in Honest and Just Business Practices*	
		PROVERBS 11:1; MICAH 2:1–3; 6:8–15	89
LESSON 10	_____	*Exulting in the Marriage Relationship*	
		GENESIS 2:18–25; HEBREWS 13:4	99
LESSON 11	_____	*Helping Children Grow*	
		PSALM 128; MATTHEW 19:13–15; EPHESIANS 6:1–4	107
LESSON 12	_____	*Being Sick and Getting Well*	
		PSALM 116; LUKE 4:38–40; JAMES 5:13–16	115
LESSON 13	_____	*Relying On God's Care When We Face Loss*	
		JOHN 11:17–26; ROMANS 8:38–39; 1 THESSALONIANS 4:13–18	125

Our Next New Study	135
Additional Future Adult Bible Studies	137
How to Order More Bible Study Materials	139

Introducing

Living Faith in Daily Life

We go to church, and we say we are Christians. But what difference does that make when Sunday is over—or even when Sunday is going on?

An Answer

This series of Bible study lessons is intended to help in answering that question and, more, in putting the answers into practice. The lessons deal with the biblical theme of *Living Faith in Daily Life*. The thirteen Bible lessons in the study have been selected to guide thought and provoke action on various aspects of this theme. Many subjects could have been chosen beyond these thirteen, but these thirteen were selected because they deal with many of the common experiences of everyday life.

The first lesson, "Knowing God in Daily Life," serves as the touchpoint for the emphases in all of the study of *Living Faith in Daily Life*. If God is present everywhere, including in the experiences of daily life, should we not seek God's presence in all of those experiences?

From there, the lessons explore various areas where we often need help in applying our faith to real life. These areas include working (lesson 2), resting (lesson 3), enjoying life (lesson 4), building community (lesson 5), showing hospitality (lesson 6), forgiving (lesson 7), dealing with money (lesson 8), being honest in business practices (lesson 9), enjoying marriage (lesson 10), guiding children (lesson 11), being sick and getting well (lesson 12), and dealing with grief and loss (lesson 13).

Do we need guidance and encouragement for "Living Faith in Daily Life" in more areas than these? Definitely. Do we need guidance and encouragement in *these* areas? Absolutely.

Studying a Biblical Theme

Ordinarily, our BaptistWay® adult Bible studies deal with lessons from one or more Bible books, following the contours of the book itself. We believe that is an excellent way of doing Bible study, and we will continue emphasizing that approach. An occasional study of a biblical theme, though, can also be a helpful part of the study diet of an adult Bible study class. Studying a biblical theme provides an opportunity to consider the theme across more than one book and, indeed, across both Testaments.

LIVING FAITH IN DAILY LIFE

Lesson 1	Knowing God in Daily Life	Psalm 139:1–12, 23–24; Proverbs 3:5–6
Lesson 2	Working with Heart	Exodus 35:30–35; Proverbs 6:6–11; Colossians 3:23–24; 2 Thessalonians 3:10–13
Lesson 3	Saying Yes to Sabbath Rest	Deuteronomy 5:12–15; Psalm 127:1–2; Mark 6:30–32
Lesson 4	Enjoying the Life God Gives	Psalm 16:7–11; Ecclesiastes 5:18–21; Luke 7:31–35
Lesson 5	Building Community	2 Kings 7:3–9, 16; Nehemiah 2:17–18; 4:6; Luke 10:25–37
Lesson 6	Welcoming (Even) the Stranger	Deuteronomy 10:17–19; Matthew 25:34–40; Luke 14:12–14; Hebrews 13:1–2
Lesson 7	Forgiving the Person Who Hurt You	Matthew 6:12, 14–15; 18:21–35; Colossians 3:12–14
Lesson 8	Setting Right Priorities in a Money-Centered World	Luke 12:15–31; 1 Timothy 6:6–10, 17–19
Lesson 9	Engaging in Honest and Just Business Practices	Proverbs 11:1; Micah 2:1–3; 6:8–15
Lesson 10	Exulting in the Marriage Relationship	Genesis 2:18–25; Hebrews 13:4

Lesson 11	Helping Children Grow	Psalm 128; Matthew 19:13–15; Ephesians 6:1–4
Lesson 12	Being Sick and Getting Well	Psalm 116; Luke 4:38–40; James 5:13–16
Lesson 13	Relying On God's Care When We Face Loss	John 11:17–26; Romans 8:38–39; 1 Thessalonians 4:13–18

LESSON ONE
Knowing God in Daily Life

FOCAL TEXTS
Psalm 139:1–12, 23–24; Proverbs 3:5–6

BACKGROUND
Psalm 139; Proverbs 3:5–6

MAIN IDEA
Since God can be counted on to be present in daily life, we are to seek God's presence there.

QUESTION TO EXPLORE
How is it possible to experience God in the worlds of work, community, and home, even in every moment of daily life?

STUDY AIM
To identify how I can experience God in the affairs of daily life

QUICK READ
Since God is present with us, we should be present to him, giving him our attention and trusting him with our lives.

Can you hear me now? That's the familiar tag line from the commercials of a cell phone company. The ads feature a man asking this question while speaking on a cell phone in various obscure places. The message is that this company can keep you in touch wherever you are.

This advertising has been effective on me because I use this company. I live in the Smoky Mountains, an area that challenges all cell phone providers. My service has been good, but I've been in a few places where if I asked that question—*Can you hear me now?*—on my cell, no one could! While this company provides excellent coverage overall, it isn't perfect. Despite its best efforts, it can't be everywhere.

This lesson's texts tell us of the God who is everywhere. He isn't limited by time or space, and so we're never out of touch with him. As we explore these texts, we'll discover that since God is present with us everywhere and at all times, we should seek God everywhere and at all times.[1]

Psalm 139:1–12, 23–24

[1] O Lord, you have searched me
   and you know me.
[2] You know when I sit and when I rise;
   you perceive my thoughts from afar.
[3] You discern my going out and my lying down;
   you are familiar with all my ways.
[4] Before a word is on my tongue
   you know it completely, O Lord.
[5] You hem me in—behind and before;
   you have laid your hand upon me.
[6] Such knowledge is too wonderful for me,
   too lofty for me to attain.
[7] Where can I go from your Spirit?
   Where can I flee from your presence?
[8] If I go up to the heavens, you are there;
   if I make my bed in the depths, you are there.
[9] If I rise on the wings of the dawn,
   if I settle on the far side of the sea,

Lesson 1: *Knowing God in Daily Life*

> ¹⁰ even there your hand will guide me,
>   your right hand will hold me fast.
> ¹¹ If I say, "Surely the darkness will hide me
>   and the light become night around me,"
> ¹² even the darkness will not be dark to you;
>   the night will shine like the day,
>   for darkness is as light to you.
>
> . . . .
>
> ²³ Search me, O God, and know my heart;
>   test me and know my anxious thoughts.
> ²⁴ See if there is any offensive way in me,
>   and lead me in the way everlasting.
>
> ## Proverbs 3:5–6
>
> ⁵ Trust in the LORD with all your heart
>   and lean not on your own understanding;
> ⁶ in all your ways acknowledge him,
>   and he will make your paths straight.

God Knows Us Intimately (Psalm 139:1–6)

A couple of years ago, I had to go through a battery of medical tests. They weren't fun, but they were amazing. Physicians now have incredible technology that enables them to probe inside our bodies without surgery. They can use X-rays, scopes, blood tests, and the like to reveal our internal organs. But none of their instruments can reveal our souls. Only God can do that.

Psalm 139:1–6 tells us that God knows us intimately. Verse 1 begins with the assertion that God has seen into the psalmist's innermost being. The word used for "know" refers to more than knowledge of facts. It refers to intimate relational knowledge. People may know facts about you, including such things as your home town, height, and weight, but they don't truly know you until they know you relationally. To do that they must spend time with you, speaking with you and observing you.

Even then, they won't know who you are deep in your soul. Only God knows us this way.

In verses 2–3 the psalmist continued speaking about this intimate knowledge by saying that God knew everything the psalmist did in the course of the day. God knew when the psalmist got up in the morning and when he lay down to sleep at night. He knew when he was working, playing, and worshiping.

The writer extended the images of God's knowledge in verses 4–6, saying that even before he spoke a word, God knew what that word would be. God limited him in a protective fashion, the way a shepherd hems in his sheep, to keep him out of danger. God laid his hand on him, not for punishment, but for protection and power. The psalmist admitted he could never know God or another human being the way God knew him. Such knowledge was too great for the psalmist to attain.

The fact that God knows us this intimately is both intimidating and reassuring. It's intimidating because God knows everything that goes on in our inner worlds. Each of us has an inner world that no other human can enter or peer into. Have you ever been shocked to learn that someone you thought you knew had done something terrible? That terrible thing was in that person's heart, but no human could see it. No human can see into your inner world, and you can't see into anyone else's. But God can. He knows both your actions and your motivations. He knows every unworthy thought.

Such knowledge can make us uncomfortable. Yet God's intimate knowledge of our inner worlds is also reassuring. He knows our joy, sorrow, pleasure, pain, faith, and doubts. God understands us fully.

God knows us and yet still loves us! As one teacher said, "He loves us, warts and all!" This knowledge should give us assurance, not fear.

God Is with Us Everywhere (Psalm 139:7–12)

While verses 1–6 focus on God's intimate knowledge of our inner worlds, verses 7–12 focus on God's presence wherever we go. As we consider these verses, it's helpful to know how ancient people viewed the universe. They believed the earth was a flat disk that rested on pillars over chaotic waters. In the earth was *Sheol*, the abode of the dead. It was like a large cave or hole in the ground. In fact, some called it the *ditch* or *pit* (see Ps. 28:1). The Hebrews believed the sky was a solid dome, and above the sky was heaven, where God lived.

In verse 7, we see that with this view of the universe in mind the psalmist asked the rhetorical questions, "Where can I go from your Spirit? Where can I flee from your presence?" He didn't express the desire to get away from God, but he was wondering where he would go if he wanted to flee from God.

In verses 8–10 he pondered God's presence in the boundaries of the universe as he understood it. In verse 8 he spoke of the height and depth of the universe: heaven and *Sheol*. It's not striking that God is present in heaven. But God's presence in *Sheol* is unexpected. Yet the psalmist said that God would be present with him even in the abode of the dead. Even in the place of greatest despair, God is near.

Verses 9–10 explore the horizontal boundaries of the universe. The psalmist said that even if he went to the farthest limits of the sea, God would be with him. The Israelites weren't a seagoing people, and so the sea was mysterious and fearsome. To go to the farthest limits of the sea was to go to strange and unknown places. Even there, though, the psalmist knew God would be with him.

Night was more intimidating for ancient people than it generally is for us. They considered it evil and frightening. People could get lost in the darkness, and their friends and family members couldn't find them. Verses 11–12 say that darkness isn't a problem for God. It's like light to him.

A VIEW OF THE UNIVERSE

The ancient Hebrews didn't see the universe as we do. They believed the earth was a flat disk resting on pillars above chaotic waters. The sky was a solid dome that held the sun, moon, and stars. Above the sky were chambers of water, and above the chambers of water was heaven, where God and the heavenly beings lived.

Too, the ancient Hebrews believed that underground, in the earth, was *Sheol*, the abode of the dead. All the dead—rich and poor, good and evil—went to *Sheol*. There they lived as *shadows* of their former selves.[2]

Psalm 139 affirms that God is present everywhere in the universe, even in the abode of the dead.

These verses assure us that no matter what our location or circumstances, God is with us. If we're at church, at work, at a football game, or at a shopping mall, God is with us. If we're going into surgery, if we're facing a crisis, or if our hearts are broken, God is also with us.

God Leads Us in the Everlasting Way (Psalm 139:23–24)

The psalm climaxes in verses 23–24 with a heartfelt cry to God. Based on God's intimate knowledge and his presence everywhere, the psalmist asked God to search him and know his heart. Ancient people used the word "heart" much in the same way we use the word *self*. We think of the heart as a person's emotional center. They thought of the heart as a person's emotional *and* cognitive center. "Heart" referred to their inner world. So when the psalmist asked God to know his heart, he was asking God to probe his innermost being.

When I took a guided tour of Carlsbad Caverns in New Mexico, the ranger had us all sit down on benches at one point. When everyone was seated, he told us he was going to show us how dark the cave was without light. After he turned off the lights, I couldn't see my hand in front of my face. It was the darkest dark I've ever experienced.

A person's heart can be just as dark and inaccessible to others. But God can see into it clearly. The psalmist asked God to shine his light into the deepest reaches of his heart to see whether there was any wicked way in him. His goal was to obey God from the inside out. He also asked God to test him and know his anxious thoughts. He wanted God to know his inner anxiety as he sought to deal with life's challenges.

Further, the psalmist wanted God to see whether there was any offensive way in him. Just as a modern surgeon would use modern technology to remove a malignant growth, the psalmist wanted God to probe in his soul and remove any sin, any spiritual malignancy. Since God was with him in all his daily activity, he wanted God to lead him in the way everlasting. "The way everlasting" refers to the way that leads to life.

Here, the psalmist gets at the heart of the spiritual life. The aim of the spiritual life is deep communion with God. This communion takes place as we become increasingly aware of God's presence and allow God to shine his light of revelation in our inner world. As we commune with God in this way, God shows us how he wants us to live.

LESSON 1: *Knowing God in Daily Life* 19

> ## FOR THOUGHT
> A person has a ticket to get on an airliner but is detained and unable to board. The airliner crashes, and all on board die in the crash. Someone says, *God must have been with the person who missed the plane.* What do you think about that statement? Does it mean God wasn't with those on the plane?

God Calls Us to Trust Him (Proverbs 3:5–6)

Proverbs 3:5–6 calls us to build on our relationships with God by trusting in the Lord with all our hearts. We can paraphrase verse 5 by saying that *we are to trust God with all our selves, with all that we are*. We're not to rely on our own insight or understanding because God's knowledge is infinitely greater than our own.

Since God is with us wherever we go, we should acknowledge him in all our ways. Not long ago I took a spiritual study course that spoke of being present to God. The idea of being present to God intrigued me. To be present to God is to be continually aware of God. It is knowing that God is with us and being attentive to God's presence.

Sometimes we're in physical proximity to others, but we're not present to them. For example, when we're sitting down at the dinner table with our families, we can be physically present with them but our minds can be elsewhere. The same can be true in our relationships with God. He's always spiritually present with us, but we're not always spiritually present to him. We're absorbed in whatever is concerning us in the moment.

The psalmist says that if we're present to God, if we acknowledge God and follow God's directions in all our ways, God will straighten and smooth our paths. He will straighten the curves, even the grades, and fill in the potholes!

Implications and Actions

Probably every person reading these comments is busy, very busy. We have jobs to do, church functions to attend, homes to clean, classes to attend, and much more. We can become so absorbed in our busyness that we lose touch with God.

How do we maintain our contact with God? We begin by knowing that God knows us intimately. He reads our souls. We continue by knowing God is with us everywhere. God is with us when we get up in the morning, when we go to work, when we return home in the evening, and when we lie down to sleep at night. On our part, we are to seek to be present to God in all we do each day, cultivating our relationship with him.

QUESTIONS

1. How do you feel about God's intimate knowledge of you? Do you find it intimidating or assuring?

2. When is it easiest for you to feel God's presence? When is it most difficult?

3. How do you feel about asking God to look deeply into your soul and reveal your offensive ways?

4. How can you increase your trust in God?

NOTES

1. Unless otherwise indicated, all Scripture quotations in lessons 1–7, 10–11 are from the New International Version.
2. By Jesus' time, Jews believed *Sheol* was divided into two sections: *Paradise*, the place of the righteous dead; and *Gehenna*, or hell, the place of the wicked dead. A huge chasm separated the two (see Luke 16:19–31).

LESSON TWO
Working with Heart

FOCAL TEXTS
Exodus 35:30–35;
Proverbs 6:6–11;
Colossians 3:23–24;
2 Thessalonians 3:10–13

BACKGROUND
Exodus 35:30–35;
Proverbs 6:6–11;
Colossians 3:23–24;
2 Thessalonians 3:10–13

MAIN IDEA
Work and work skills are God-given and provide an opportunity for serving the Lord.

QUESTIONS TO EXPLORE
How is God related to your work? How is your work related to God?

STUDY AIM
To develop ways for relating what I do in life to God and God's purposes

QUICK READ
God gives us our work skills to provide for our needs. We should serve God through our work.

"Hands to work, hearts to God." That was a motto of the Shakers, a religious group that arrived in America about the time of the Revolutionary War. Shakers believed that their mission was to participate in God's mission of redeeming the world. They sought to do so through the skillful labor of their hands. They put their devotion to God into what they made, believing that God worked in the details and the quality of their labor. They meticulously constructed and maintained their villages, and their products were world-famous for their quality and craftsmanship.[1]

In the Shaker faith, work was an expression of worship and redemption. This concept is largely foreign to us. We tend to see only certain kinds of work as *sacred*. For example, when I was in seminary, a new student enrolled who had been a top executive at a major American corporation. He left his job, though, to pursue a career in vocational Christian ministry. He did so because he stated that he wanted to "work for God." Perhaps his pursuing vocational Christian ministry was indeed what God wanted him to do. Even so, the statement can be taken to imply that only those who engage in vocational Christian ministry "work for God." Such an attitude is common among Christians. We often divide work into *secular* and *sacred* categories. Thus we think secular work includes being an executive at a major corporation. Sacred work includes being a pastor or missionary.

We use the word "call" almost exclusively in relation to church-related careers. We tend not to use it in relation to other kinds of work. Some of us struggle to find any connection between our work and God.

In today's texts, we'll find that our first calling is to follow Christ, and that our work should be an expression of that calling.

EXODUS 35:30–35

30 Then Moses said to the Israelites, "See, the Lord has chosen Bezalel son of Uri, the son of Hur, of the tribe of Judah, **31** and he has filled him with the Spirit of God, with skill, ability and knowledge in all kinds of crafts— **32** to make artistic designs for work in gold, silver and bronze, **33** to cut and set stones, to work in wood and to engage in all kinds of artistic craftsmanship. **34** And he has given both him and Oholiab son of Ahisamach, of the tribe of Dan, the ability to teach others. ³⁵ He has filled them with skill to do all kinds of work as craftsmen, designers, embroiderers in blue, purple and scarlet yarn and fine linen, and weavers—all of them master craftsmen and designers.

PROVERBS 6:6–11

⁶ Go to the ant, you sluggard;
  consider its ways and be wise!
⁷ It has no commander,
  no overseer or ruler,
⁸ yet it stores its provisions in summer
  and gathers its food at harvest.
⁹ How long will you lie there, you sluggard?
  When will you get up from your sleep?
¹⁰ A little sleep, a little slumber,
  a little folding of the hands to rest—
¹¹ and poverty will come on you like a bandit
  and scarcity like an armed man.

COLOSSIANS 3:23–24

²³ Whatever you do, work at it with all your heart, as working for the Lord, not for men, ²⁴ since you know that you will receive an inheritance from the Lord as a reward. It is the Lord Christ you are serving.

2 THESSALONIANS 3:10–13

¹⁰ For even when we were with you, we gave you this rule: "If a man will not work, he shall not eat."

¹¹ We hear that some among you are idle. They are not busy; they are busybodies. ¹² Such people we command and urge in the Lord Jesus Christ to settle down and earn the bread they eat. ¹³ And as for you, brothers, never tire of doing what is right.

God Gives Us Work Skills (Exodus 35:30–35)

Exodus 35 tells about preparations for construction of the tabernacle during the early days of Israel's history, immediately after deliverance from Egypt. The tabernacle was Israel's portable structure for sacrifice and worship, and symbol of God's presence. Verses 30–35 speak of Bezalel and his assistant Oholiab, who were the leading craftsmen for the project. Construction of the tabernacle would require skilled workmen because its plans called for intricate carving, casting, embroidery, and the like.

Moses said in verse 30 that the Lord chose Bezalel for this work. God called this man for this task. In verse 31 Moses also said that the Lord had "filled him with the Spirit of God, with skill, ability and knowledge in all kinds of crafts." These verses express a principle we find throughout the Scriptures: God calls people to his work and gives them the ability to do it.

The work of Bezalel and Oholiab tests the distinction between sacred and secular work. Building the tabernacle was a sacred task, but it required skills that could be applied in secular ways. We normally think of gifts of God's Spirit in relation to work like preaching, teaching, prophesying, and healing. But here the text says God gifted Bezalel with the skill of a craftsman, enabling him to make beautiful things with his hands.

This means God's calling and gifting isn't limited to *church work*. God does call and provide gifts to missionaries, pastors, and other kinds of ministers. Yet God also calls and gifts attorneys, aircraft pilots, bankers, bricklayers, carpenters, executives, mechanics, nurses, physicians, teachers, and more. We often think of God empowering people to do *spiritual* things, but the case of Bezalel suggests that God empowers people to do *physical* tasks as well.

God Gives Us Work to Provide for Ourselves (Proverbs 6:6–11)

While Exodus 35:30–35 tells us that physical work has spiritual dimensions, Proverbs 6:6–11 tells us that God gives us work to provide for ourselves. The Book of Proverbs has many illustrations from the animal world. In this section, the writer focused on the common ant. Everyone

LESSON 2: *Working with Heart*

has seen an ant hill and observed the industrious nature of the species.

The writer addressed the "sluggard." A sluggard is a lazy person who has little interest in work. The proverb instructed the sluggard to consider the ant and be wise. In Proverbs, to "be wise" is to *live successfully*. It refers to negotiating life's challenges and thriving spiritually and materially.

Verses 7–8 observe that the ant has no supervisor standing over it, cracking a whip and making it work. Nonetheless, it works continually, gathering its provisions in harvest time and storing them away for the harsh winter to come.

Verse 9 speaks to the lazy sluggard, who's taking a nap instead of working. Verse 10 mocks the lazy person by repeating his motto, "A little sleep, a little slumber, a little folding of the hands to rest." Sounds like a restful, peaceful song, but verse 11 goes on to pronounce the dire warning that poverty will come on him "like a bandit," and "scarcity" like an armed robber!

The Scriptures teach that God made us to work. Genesis 2:15 tells us that God put Adam in the Garden of Eden to "work it and take care of

OCCUPATIONS IN THE BIBLE

The New Testament mentions a number of different occupations. Lowest on the social scale were slaves (Ephesians 6:5, 9). Slaves were the property of their masters and had no rights. Slightly higher were servants (see Luke 19:17), who worked for low wages. Day laborers (Matthew 20:1–16) gathered at public places hoping to be hired for various kinds of work.

Craftsmen usually learned their crafts from their fathers. The Apostle Paul was a tentmaker (Acts 18:3). Mark 6:3 records that people in Jesus' hometown called him "the carpenter," while Matthew 13:55 refers to him as "the carpenter's son." Doubtless both are correct because sons usually learned their trades from their fathers.

Women mostly labored in the home, but Acts 16:14 mentions that Lydia was "a dealer in purple cloth." The description of the ideal wife in Proverbs 31:10–31 shows that wives in the upper classes were involved in various kinds of business ventures like real estate and trading.

it." Many people think work was part of God's curse. But in truth God's curse was harsh, unfulfilling toil (Genesis 3:17–19), not work in itself.

God's plan for us is that we work for our needs. The Lord has never delivered our material needs to our doorsteps. Instead, God has given us the skill to work and provide for our needs. In truth, we can see work as part of a divine partnership. God gives us the ability to work, and we work. Then God blesses our work and provides for our needs.

We Can Serve God Through Our Work (Colossians 3:23–24)

Colossians 3:23–24 is in a section in which the Apostle Paul was addressing relationships in the Christian household. In verse 22 he spoke to slaves, urging them to obey their masters, and not just when they had their eyes on them! With the work of slaves in mind but addressing the Christian community as a whole, he wrote in verses 23–24 that believers should do whatever work they do with all their hearts. They should work as if they were working for the Lord himself, not for their earthly bosses. He emphasized that ultimately they were serving the Lord Jesus Christ through their work.

Here, as in the case of Bezalel, we have reference to what we think of as *secular* work being done in service to Christ. The work to which Paul referred wasn't *church* work in the sense that we think. It included the work of the slave, the craftsman, the soldier, the farmer, and the scribe. Similarly, at our jobs we work for more than our earthly employers. We work for the Lord Jesus himself. Whatever work we do, we should do it in service to the Lord to bring him glory.

At this point, it's appropriate to ponder the concepts of *calling* and *vocation*. Does God call us to certain careers or vocations? The Scriptures never speak of God calling people to careers. They do speak of Christ calling us to follow him (Matthew 16:24). As it's stated in the book, *Go to Work and Take Your Faith Too!*

> Your work in itself is not your calling. Your calling is to be a Christian. Your work, however, may well be—or can be—an *expression* of your calling to be a person of faith. Your daily work can be a means by which you seek to act day by day in partnership with God's purposes.[2]

LESSON 2: *Working with Heart* 27

This gets us back to the Shaker concept of work. They saw their work as an expression of their service to God, as an act of worship and redemption.

We Should Work for Our Daily Bread (2 Thessalonians 3:10–13)

In 2 Thessalonians 3, the Apostle Paul warned his readers against idleness. In verses 8–10, he pointed to the example of his own life. We know that Paul was a "tentmaker" by trade (Acts 18:3) and that he supported himself by the work of his hands. He reminded the Thessalonians that when he was among them, he worked day and night, preaching the gospel and working at his tentmaking trade. He made his own money so he wouldn't be a burden on the church.

In verse 10, Paul reminded them of what he taught while he was with them, "If a man will not work, he shall not eat." In his mind, there was no excuse for able-bodied people to refuse to work.

Paul continued in verses 11–12 by saying that he had heard that some within the church were idle. Instead of being "busy," they were "busybodies," gossiping and creating discontent in the church. The old saying is true, "Idle hands are the devil's workshop." When we're idle, not engaged in constructive work, we can have unworthy thoughts and do unworthy things.

Paul commanded the idle to "settle down" and earn what they ate. He wanted them to be productive and not burden the church. They were to labor at doing right and not grow weary of it.

GOD'S WILL AND WORK

A member of your class comes to you and says she is wondering whether she's doing God's will in her work. She's a commercial banker who makes loans to businesses. She's basically happy in her work and performs it with integrity. Yet she wants to serve God in her work and doesn't sense God's presence in what she does. She asks you whether God may be calling her to fulltime Christian service, like international mission work.

How would you counsel her? What Scriptures do you think would relate to her struggle?

God made us for productive work. He arranged life so we would have to work for our bread. When we don't work, we lose the blessing of earning our bread, and we open ourselves to many problems and temptations. In the Christian community, it's important that we all be engaged in work so we can support ourselves and focus on serving Christ.

Implications and Actions

In our day, we Christians are tempted to over-emphasize work and also to completely separate work from our relationship with God. Our first calling is to follow him as Lord and Savior. After that, we should seek God's calling in every area of our lives, including our work.

We gain much of our sense of self-worth from our work. Even so, although our work is important, it shouldn't define us. Sometimes when we lose our jobs or retire, we can lapse into depression because we've lost a critical aspect of our lives. But what defines us is our relationship to God through the Lord Jesus Christ. We should find our sense of self-worth through that relationship. Even when we lose paid work, we can still be engaged in volunteer work, finding fulfillment in serving others.

Our work is an expression of our response to Christ's call to follow him. For this reason, we should work as if Christ were our boss and do the best quality work we can do with high integrity and ethics. We can see our work as part of our worship and our redemptive partnership with God.

LESSON 2: *Working with Heart*

QUESTIONS

1. What skills do you believe God has given you for work? How are you using those skills?

2. What difficulties do you have working under supervisors at work? How would your difficulties change if you saw yourself as working for Christ?

3. What if you were unable to work any longer? How could you still serve Christ?

4. How would it change your work and your attitudes toward it if you saw it as an expression of your worship of God and your participation in God's redemptive work?

NOTES

1. "Shaker." *Encyclopædia Britannica*. 2010. Encyclopædia Britannica Online. <http://www.britannica.com/EBchecked/topic/537839/Shakers>. Accessed 1/28/2010.
2. Ross West, *Go to Work and Take Your Faith Too!* (Macon, Georgia: Smyth and Helwys, 1997), 29–30 (italics in original).

LESSON THREE
Saying Yes to Sabbath Rest

FOCAL TEXTS
Deuteronomy 5:12–15;
Psalm 127:1–2;
Mark 6:30–32

BACKGROUND
Exodus 20:8–11;
Deuteronomy 5:12–15;
Psalm 127;
Mark 4:35–41; 6:30–32

MAIN IDEA
Rest, like work, is part of God's plan for human life.

QUESTION TO EXPLORE
Are we so driven by both work and recreation that we fail to say yes to the Sabbath rest?

STUDY AIM
To decide how I will apply these teachings on the Sabbath rest to my life

QUICK READ
God calls us to say yes to Sabbath rest by stopping, resting, and communing with him.

When I was a child, Sunday was my favorite day. It started with sleeping a little later than usual, followed by getting up and putting on my Sunday clothes. After that, our family rode in our car to church. My first activity was Sunday School. There I learned Bible verses like "Love one another" (John 13:34) and songs like "Praise Him, Praise Him."[1] Following that was worship in *big church*. During worship we sang hymns like "The Solid Rock."[2] Of course there was the sermon, during which I either drew pictures on the bulletin or stared up at the rafters and chandeliers!

Going to church was great, but what came after was even better! Our family joined my great-grandmother, grandparents, aunts, uncles, and cousins at my great-grandmother's house. After changing from our Sunday clothes into our play clothes, we feasted on a meal of fried chicken, mashed potatoes, gravy, homemade biscuits, and sweet tea. Then we topped it all off with chocolate cake or peach cobbler. Energized by the meal, my cousins and I had rousing adventures in the yard all afternoon while the grownups napped.

Those were Sabbaths! They included worship, rest, feasting, visiting with family, and play. Sadly, they don't happen like this in my extended family anymore. My great-grandmother passed away many years ago. My parents got divorced, along with many of my uncles and aunts. We cousins live far away from one another and see one another only at funerals. Our children will never experience the Sundays that we did.

In this lesson, we'll explore the idea of saying yes to Sabbath rest. We tend to be busy, driven people who have a difficult time stopping, resting, and communing with God and one another. We'll see that we're missing much by turning away from saying yes to Sabbath rest as God designed it.

DEUTERONOMY 5:12–15

[12] "Observe the Sabbath day by keeping it holy, as the LORD your God has commanded you. [13] Six days you shall labor and do all your work, [14] but the seventh day is a Sabbath to the LORD your God. On it you shall not do any work, neither you, nor your son or daughter, nor your manservant or maidservant, nor your ox, your donkey or any of your animals, nor the alien within your

Lesson 3: *Saying Yes to Sabbath Rest*

gates, so that your manservant and maidservant may rest, as you do. ¹⁵ Remember that you were slaves in Egypt and that the LORD your God brought you out of there with a mighty hand and an outstretched arm. Therefore the LORD your God has commanded you to observe the Sabbath day.

PSALM 127:1–2

¹ Unless the LORD builds the house,
  its builders labor in vain.
Unless the LORD watches over the city,
  the watchmen stand guard in vain.
² In vain you rise early
  and stay up late,
toiling for food to eat—
  for he grants sleep to those he loves.

MARK 6:30–32

³⁰ The apostles gathered around Jesus and reported to him all they had done and taught. ³¹ Then, because so many people were coming and going that they did not even have a chance to eat, he said to them, "Come with me by yourselves to a quiet place and get some rest."

³² So they went away by themselves in a boat to a solitary place.

God's Command to Stop, Commune with Him, and Rest (Deuteronomy 5:12–15)

The Book of Deuteronomy describes how Moses reviewed God's laws with the Israelites before they entered Canaan. Deuteronomy 5:6–21 presents what we call the Ten Commandments. The first four commands focus on our relationship with God. The first (Deuteronomy 5:7) says we're to worship only God. The second (Deut. 5:8–10) says we're not to make an idol. The third (5:11) says we're not to take the name of God lightly or in an empty manner. The fourth (5:12–15) says God's people are to remember the Sabbath day by keeping it holy.

In Hebrew, the word "Sabbath" comes from a root meaning *to stop*. Its basic idea is ceasing activity. The Sabbath day in the Hebrew week ran from sunset Friday to sunset Saturday. The command says to keep or observe the Sabbath day by keeping it holy. In Hebrew, the word "holy" means *set apart*. The Israelites were to keep the Sabbath day holy by setting it apart to God for rest and communion with him.

The command says God's people were to labor six days. As we saw last week, God gave us labor as a means to serve God and provide for our needs. But the seventh day was to be a Sabbath, a cessation of activity dedicated to the Lord.

Verse 14b says God's people were not to limit the day's rest to themselves. They were to extend it to their children, their servants, aliens, and even their animals. God showed his claim on all living things through the Sabbath.

The motivation for the Sabbath differs in Exodus and Deuteronomy. Exodus 20:11 says:

> For in six days the LORD made the heavens and the earth, the sea, and all that is in them, but he rested on the seventh day. Therefore the LORD blessed the Sabbath day and made it holy.

This passage suggests that the Sabbath is to remind God's people of God's creation of the universe (see Genesis 2:2–3). The passage sets the Sabbath in the rhythm of God's work. If God needs a rest, humanity certainly does! In contrast, Deuteronomy 5:15 draws attention to the fact that God rescued his people from slavery in Egypt. Exodus emphasizes God's creation while Deuteronomy emphasizes God's re-creation or redemption of his people.

Celebration of the Sabbath became one of the distinctive practices of the Jews. By Jesus' time it had become a restrictive, highly legalistic practice. Conflict erupted between Jesus and Jewish leadership, especially the Pharisees, over Sabbath practices (see Matthew 12:1–12). Jesus reminded them that God established the Sabbath for humanity. He didn't create humanity for the Sabbath (Mark 2:27).

LESSON 3: *Saying Yes to Sabbath Rest*

The Limits of Labor (Psalm 127:1–2)

An important lesson of the Sabbath is that labor has limits. Psalm 127 emphasizes God's power and sovereignty. The first part of verse 1 says that unless the Lord builds the house, its builders build in vain. If God isn't in the construction, no amount of skill, labor, or precaution will keep the house standing. The second part of verse 1 says that unless the Lord watches over the city, its watchmen watch in vain. Leaders of ancient cities stationed watchmen on walls and in watchtowers to keep watch for the approach of an enemy. The psalmist was saying that unless the Lord watches over the city, no number of watchmen will keep it safe.

The New Revised Standard Version of verse 2 says, "It is in vain that you rise up early and go late to rest, eating the bread of anxious toil; for he gives sleep to his beloved." An alternate translation of the last clause is, "for he provides for his beloved during sleep." In lesson two, we learned that Proverbs commends hard work (Proverbs 6:6–11) and that Paul said that if people didn't work, they shouldn't eat (2 Thessalonians 3:10). But Psalm 127:2 reminds us that hard work alone doesn't ensure

WHY SUNDAY?

Why is the Christian day of worship Sunday rather than Saturday? Jesus observed the traditional Jewish Sabbath (Mark 1:21). Most early Christians did the same. Church history records no official church decision on this matter. Instead, documents of the early church (such as the *Didache*) confirm that Christians began worshiping on Sunday early in church history. It appears that the church gradually gravitated away from Saturday, the last day of the Jewish week, to Sunday, the first day of the week. It may have done so because Jesus rose from the dead on the first day (Matthew 28:1) and because the church became predominantly Gentile. Sabbath observance was not part of Gentile culture. Some Scripture passages suggest that Christians were worshiping on Sunday as early as the New Testament era (Acts 20:7; 1 Corinthians 16:2).[3]

Not all Christian groups agree with this shift to Sunday. They maintain that God never intended the church to make Sunday its day of rest and worship. Among these are Seventh-Day Adventists and Seventh-Day Baptists.

> ### REALLY FINDING REST
>
> During a deacons meeting, a deacon raises the issue of establishing a day of rest on Sunday. One deacon laments the fact that the law allows stores and other businesses to be open on Sunday. He argues that the deacon body should lobby the state legislature to restore such laws. Another deacon says that their own church meeting schedule isn't conducive to rest. Committees meet nearly every Sunday.
>
> What perspective does each deacon bring to the issue of rest? Which approach is more likely to yield rest in this church?

our well being. God must be in our work. Sometimes we need to set our work aside and trust God for his provision.

We can work long hours, sacrifice time with our families, and expend all our energies in our labor, only to see our work come to nothing. Worse than that, we can neglect our relationships with God and our families. This psalm calls us to remember that if we don't trust in God and maintain a relationship with him, all our work can come to nothing.

The Need to Withdraw for a Time (Mark 6:30–32)

Mark 6:30–32 shows Jesus and his disciples in a busy, demanding time. Jesus' disciples had fanned out across the countryside preaching and healing (see Mark 6:7–13). They had returned to Jesus and were describing all they had done. Apparently, they had been successful, for huge crowds were gathering around them. Verse 31 says that so many people were coming and going, they didn't even have a chance to eat!

Knowing that he and his disciples couldn't keep up this pace, Jesus said to them, "Come with me by yourselves to a quiet place and get some rest"(6:31b) Although their work was critically important, Jesus knew his disciples needed rest. If they kept working as they were doing, they were going to become exhausted, perhaps to the point of illness, and ineffective.

It appears that this wasn't the only time Jesus retreated with the disciples, because Mark 4:35–41 mentions another occasion on which he took them away from the demands of the crowd. On that occasion, Jesus taught his disciples about rest and faith by calming a storm that threatened to swamp their boat while he was sleeping.

Mark 6:32 says Jesus took his disciples away to "a quiet place." The New Revised Standard Version calls it "a deserted place." They needed to go to a place where the crowds couldn't find them and they could enjoy quiet rest and reflection.

Sometimes we become so intense in our work that we think we don't have time to stop and rest. Our work seems critically important, and we think that terrible things will happen if we don't work. Yet even the Lord Jesus recognized that he and his disciples needed time to rest. What work could be more important than theirs? When we feel our work is too critical to stop, we show a lack of faith. After all, as we learned from Psalm 127, our work is in vain if God isn't in it. From time to time, we need to withdraw to a quiet place and rest. When we do so, we gain not only rest, but also perspective and restored spiritual power.

Note that Jesus took his disciples to a "quiet place." Sometimes our recreation is just as driven as our work. We plan a vacation but fill it with sightseeing and many other activities. Have you ever come home feeling you needed a vacation after your vacation? In addition to this, we spend our free time on the weekends playing baseball and soccer games, or taking our children to such activities. Our days of rest become blurs of activity that benefit us little.

In addition to our weekly Sabbath rest, we should occasionally spend time in extended retreat. We need to spend time away from crowds and the frenetic pace of constant activity and get away to a place of quiet rest. It doesn't need to be a luxury resort. Many church camps have inexpensive rooms available for individuals and families to spend time retreating and focusing on God.

Implications and Actions

The first call of the Sabbath is to *stop*. If we're working long hours, we can ask ourselves whether our efforts come from the demands of our employer or from our own ambitions. We can ask whether we're working to make a name for ourselves or to gain life's necessities.

The second call is to *rest*. Sometimes we're just as busy in our recreation as we are in our work. We can ask ourselves whether our recreation is resting us or merely burning us out further.

The third call is to *commune* with God and with others. The purpose of the Sabbath is for us to stop and give our attention to God. We can become so busy with our work and recreation that we don't make space for God. A Sabbath helps us set aside time to give our undivided attention to him. Furthermore, a Sabbath can help us give attention to our relationships with our families and our brothers and sisters in Christ. Such attention enriches both us and them.

QUESTIONS

1. In what ways can you bring reflection on God's creation and redemption into your Sabbath rest?

2. In what ways can you establish a true Sabbath in your week?

3. In what ways can you better connect with your fellow church members on Sunday?

4. In what ways can you better connect with your family on Sunday?

NOTES

1. "Praise Him, All Ye Little Children," words anonymous.
2. "My Hope Is Built," words by Edward Mote (about 1834).
3. See www.baylor.edu/christianethics/Sabbathstudyguide3.pdf.

LESSON FOUR
Enjoying the Life God Gives

FOCAL TEXTS
Psalm 16:7–11;
Ecclesiastes 5:18–20;
Luke 7:31–35

BACKGROUND
Psalm 16;
Ecclesiastes 5:18–20;
Luke 7:31–35

MAIN IDEA
When we follow God's path of life, we find fullness of joy.

QUESTION TO EXPLORE
How can Christians be known more as people of genuine joy rather than as killjoys?

STUDY AIM
To identify ways my joy in life can be increased

QUICK READ
When God is allowed to move freely in our lives, joy happens. Joy is natural to the Christian experience, but we can either magnify its impact or impede its flow.

Two women were chatting on the phone. One remarked, "You don't seem quite yourself today. Did you wake up grumpy?"

The other said, "No, I let him sleep."

Such is life. Sometimes we wake up on the wrong side of the bed, and sometimes that happens to another. What about *our* disposition? What about joy and grumpiness? Can we try to retreat from our grumpiness by saying, *I was born that way*, or *it's not my fault; she (or he) always makes me feel this way*? Can we do something about the way we act and react? Can we really become joyous? The Bible teaches we can. As the Scripture unfolds, note how joy can be experienced and encouraged.

PSALM 16:7–11

7 I will praise the LORD, who counsels me;
   even at night my heart instructs me.
8 I have set the LORD always before me.
   Because he is at my right hand,
   I will not be shaken.
9 Therefore my heart is glad and my tongue rejoices;
   my body also will rest secure,
10 because you will not abandon me to the grave,
    nor will you let your Holy One see decay.
11 You have made known to me the path of life;
    you will fill me with joy in your presence,
    with eternal pleasures at your right hand.

ECCLESIASTES 5:18–20

18 Then I realized that it is good and proper for a man to eat and drink, and to find satisfaction in his toilsome labor under the sun during the few days of life God has given him—for this is his lot. 19 Moreover, when God gives any man wealth and possessions, and enables him to enjoy them, to accept his lot and be happy in his work—this is a gift of God. 20 He seldom reflects on the days of his life, because God keeps him occupied with gladness of heart.

LESSON 4: *Enjoying the Life God Gives*

> ## LUKE 7:31–35
>
> ³¹ "To what, then, can I compare the people of this generation? What are they like? ³² They are like children sitting in the marketplace and calling out to each other:
>
> "'We played the flute for you,
>   and you did not dance;
> we sang a dirge,
>   and you did not cry.'
>
> ³³ For John the Baptist came neither eating bread nor drinking wine, and you say, 'He has a demon.' ³⁴ The Son of Man came eating and drinking, and you say, 'Here is a glutton and a drunkard, a friend of tax collectors and "sinners."' ³⁵ But wisdom is proved right by all her children."

Joy Is Where God Is (Psalm 16:7–11)

David is a leading figure in the Old Testament, but even a casual reading of the Psalms and Old Testament history reveals that David had both his good and bad moments. He wrestled with the guilt of his sin concerning Bathsheba and Uriah (Psalms 32 and 51), but Psalms is also filled with his praise of God and rejoicing in who God is and what God has done. Although David is described as a person "who enjoyed God's favor" (Acts 7:46), we know that David had characteristics in common with us. We all have our moments when we are not our best. Psalm 16, however, is a prayer song that describes David feeling his best about God.

The psalmist wrote, "In Your presence is fullness of joy" (Ps. 16:11, NASB). What do you think of when you think of God? Some think of love, and others of judgment. Some imagine God as a benevolent grandparent, and some as a stern taskmaster. Many images may have some appropriateness. In Psalm 16, however, David confessed his faith in God and acknowledged that God had brought meaning and great pleasure to his life. David had come to the point where God was the *joy-maker* of his life.

Grace and faith are revealed in this prayer and song. Think about David's testimony to the grace of God:
- God revealed wisdom to David (16:7).
- David believed God took care of him in life and would not abandon him in death (16:9–10). Perhaps David understood even more about death than his fellow Hebrews knew at this point. He had confidence God would not abandon him in death or *Sheol* (in Hebrew thought, a place for the dead) with no hope for a meaningful eternity.
- The psalm closes with David's belief that God had revealed the right way for David to live and great joy had come into his life (16:11).

In David's response to who God is and what God had done, notice David's actions of faith in the psalm. Are any of these outside the realm of possibility for you?
- David praised God (16:7).
- He stayed aware that he was always in the presence of God (16:8).
- He was happy and secure with God (16:9).
- He had hope in God for this life and eternity (16:10).
- He enjoyed the pleasures of belonging to God. He was filled with joy (16:11).

Grace and faith are good companions (see Ephesians 2:8–10). God's grace and David's faith led David to experience the fullness of joy. Unlike David, you may not be able to say "I have set the Lord always before me" or "my heart is glad and my tongue rejoices" (16:8–9). We all have our moments when we are not at the top of our spiritual lives. If you are not, just admit it. Then, get back to being the person you can be. Only David can be David, and only you can be you. The good things that happened to David can also happen to you and me.

It's OK to Enjoy Life (Ecclesiastes 5:18–20)

In some respects, Ecclesiastes presents a pessimistic, negative view of life. "Meaningless! Meaningless! . . . Utterly meaningless! Everything is meaningless!" is the way the book begins (Ecclesiastes 1:2). Yet,

LESSON 4: *Enjoying the Life God Gives*

following that introduction, many pearls of truth are appropriate to New Testament Christianity. Ecclesiastes 5:18–20 embraces the quest for authentic enjoyment of life.

This section of Scripture is alluded to in a parable of Jesus in Luke 12:13–21. The parable is known as the parable of the rich fool, a man who decided to "eat, drink and be merry" (Luke 12:20). The man's problem was not that he planned to enjoy life. His problem was that he was going to do so in a selfish way, ignoring God and his fellow human beings. Notice how many times the first person pronouns of *I, me, my* and *mine* are used by the rich fool in only two verses—Luke 12:18–19.

Now, back to Ecclesiastes. In several other portions of the book (Eccles. 2:24–25; 3:12–13, 22; 8:15; 9:7–10; and 11:7–10), we see similar encouragement to enjoy life. It really is okay to enjoy things, possessions,

---

IMPARTING JOY TO OTHERS

Grady Nutt was a Baptist preacher, but he was famous as an entertainer who brought joy to many people. Among other things, he was the author of several books, a speaker at many Baptist student gatherings, and a member of the cast of the television show *Hee Haw*. He died in a plane crash in 1982.

My wife and I knew him in Texas and Kentucky, arriving at Baylor University and Southern Seminary just a little later at both places than he did. He spoke at a Christmas banquet at our church in Atlanta, Georgia. We laughed until we cried and ached!

Grady had a great mind and a big heart. He was funny, with big eyes, big hands, and a big smile. Everything about him was *Texas-sized*. He could play and sing, and his stories were often from everyday life. He said there was no need to make up stories, for life was full of them if you would just see them. Grady's *joy quotient* was really high![1]

There was only one Grady Nutt, but we too can impart joy to others. We can take ourselves less seriously and selfishly, laugh at ourselves, and laugh with others. Much of life would be brighter and happier if more people did that. Yes, I'm grateful for the profound preachers and great theologians, but I am also thankful for faithful people who can make people smile and laugh, and thus bring joy to the lives of others.

and life. The problems come when we ignore the abundant teaching of Scripture to use our possessions for glorifying God, building up the church, and meeting the needs of other people. Unfortunately, many succumb to the rich fool's love of things and pleasure for selfish indulgence, rather than enjoying life in the context of honoring God and caring for others.

Ecclesiastes has a tone within it of *go ahead and enjoy life, for it's pretty miserable anyway*. That is not the Christian approach to life. We enjoy life and possessions for good reasons, while embracing in theory and practice the fuller teaching of the Bible concerning the use of our possessions. Stewardship is the theological word for this truth, and it simply means we manage on behalf of God all that we have. When we do this properly, we will help maximize joy, not only for ourselves but also for others.

Can Anybody Catch Happiness from You? (Luke 7:31–35)

Jesus had more problems with religious leaders than he did with ordinary people. Consider the experience of Matthew, a tax-collector. Do you remember what a man named Levi did when Jesus called him to be a disciple? He threw a party. It was such a big event, he wanted to share it with his friends—and Jesus came too (Luke 5:27–30)! The religious leaders ("Pharisees and the teachers of the law") were around, too,

---

JUST FOR FUN

Leisure and sports are big factors in our world. Sometimes, they exercise almost god-like control among their practitioners and devotees. We can become so obsessed with them we forget that our recreation should be fun and enjoyable. Children at a young age are gearing up to be professional athletes, with tough practices to prepare them for bigger venues and opportunities. Whatever happened to playing for fun, enjoying a table game with your family, or hiking for the beauty of the walk? Do we really have to work at our play? What can you do to instill joy and fun in playing games, experiencing a vacation, and just hanging out with family and friends?

complaining that Jesus was partying with tax collectors and sinners. People like that are always watching.

Later in Luke 7, Jesus saluted John the Baptist as a great spiritual leader, but then he pointed out that the religious leaders would embrace neither John nor himself. To make his point, Jesus told a parable of children playing games. When happy music was played, nobody wanted to dance. When the suggestion was made that they play funeral, no child wanted to do that either. The implication was that nothing could please them. Jesus used that simple illustration to point out that the religious leaders just didn't get it. They would not embrace John the Baptist, his strange dress and diet, as well as his tough preaching talk. They thought he was crazy. They would not embrace Jesus either, because they thought Jesus partied and associated with the wrong kind of people. God was revealing something great about himself in John and Jesus, and the religious elite were too biased and self-centered to see.

Jesus led a disciplined life, but he also enjoyed life. The Jesus who died on the cross also did his first miracle at a wedding reception (John 2) and said on the day before his crucifixion, "be of good cheer, I have overcome the world" (John 16:33, Revised Standard Version). Jesus made it possible for others, including us, to have the greatest reasons for joy that anyone could have. Like Jesus, we too can help people experience joy. When we make it possible for others to experience joy or a greater joy, our joy will increase as well.

Jesus crossed paths with many people in his short ministry. Legalistic, tradition-bound, and self-righteous religious leaders could not stand Jesus, but these verses reveal a dark side to the opposition. Think about it: Jesus' critics were complaining because Jesus was too happy and free, socializing with the wrong kind of people. Apparently, the religious leaders thought they had higher standards than Jesus. Such pride and self-righteousness goes a long way in stifling expressions of joy and enthusiasm, even in the twenty-first century.

Jesus' closing words, "nevertheless, wisdom is vindicated by all her children" (Luke 7:35, New Revised Standard Version), could be simply a proverbial saying similar to our saying, "The proof is in the pudding." However, it could also mean that Jesus was confident that history would prove him to be right, and part of the evidence would be in the lives of those who followed him.

> ## Time to Throw a Party?
>
> What does your church do to celebrate a person's conversion and baptism? Are families encouraged to have a party over life's greatest decision? That certainly seems to be a great time to have a party!
>
> You throw the party, and I believe Jesus will show up—along with a minister or two, maybe some unchurched family and friends. Who knows what can happen when our joy overflows into a celebration?

Applying This Lesson to Life

Happiness and joy are different. The root word of happiness is *hap*, and it pertains to chance or circumstances. Thus, if our circumstances are not good, we are not happy. Some circumstances in this world make happiness virtually impossible. On the other hand, we can have joy regardless of the circumstances. Joy is the radiance and smile of God in the human soul. It is the disposition of God somehow shining through our lives to others. Joy is the beat of God's spiritual drums in the spirit of a human life. Joy comes from the Holy Spirit's growing the fruit of joy on our tree (Galatians 5:22). Joy is a command of God ("Rejoice in the Lord always," Philippians 4:4) and a choice we make. We can have and share joy, regardless of the circumstances.

When a prominent coach seemed to be sick, someone asked, *Does the coach have ulcers?* Someone spoke up and said, *No, but he is a carrier.* Perhaps there's more truth than fiction or humor in that statement. Some people enrich our experiences; some make life difficult for others. Some brighten our lives; others darken our lives. Some bring joy to others; others dampen others' spirits. What about you, do you bring joy or kill joy?

LESSON 4: *Enjoying the Life God Gives* 47

QUESTIONS

1. How was David's joy affected by grace and faith?

2. What would need to happen for you to be more joyous?

3. Paul wrote to the Philippians, saying "make my joy complete" (Philippians 2:2). How can you complete the joy of another person?

4. Would your friends or class say you are a joy to be with? Why or why not?

5. What kind of events should your church sponsor to encourage building fellowship and encouraging joyous experiences?

6. What implications for your church's ministry are found in Jesus' willingness to associate publicly with "tax collectors and sinners" (Luke 7:34)?

NOTES

1. See www.tshaonline.org/handbook/online/articles/NN/fnu7.html. Accessed 1/26/2010.

LESSON FIVE
Building Community

FOCAL TEXTS
2 Kings 7:3–9, 16; Nehemiah 2:17–18; 4:6; Luke 10:25–37

BACKGROUND
2 Kings 6:24—7:16; Nehemiah 2:1—4:6; Luke 10:25–37; 22:24–27

MAIN IDEA
God's people are to act so as to build community with their fellow human beings.

QUESTION TO EXPLORE
To what extent are we seeking to build community with our fellow human beings rather than isolating ourselves or acting selfishly?

STUDY AIM
To identify ways in which I will seek to build community with my fellow human beings rather than isolating myself or acting selfishly

QUICK READ
Becoming a Christian connects us as fellow citizens in the kingdom of God, as sisters and brothers in God's family. We honor God and fellow believers when we work to strengthen the ties that unite us.

When it comes to holidays, Independence Day is big—fireworks, parades, picnics, solemn observances, and ideally a day filled with thanksgiving for our nation and the freedoms it offers. The Declaration of Independence, dated July 4, 1776, declares the foundational basis for the break with Great Britain and the formation of a new nation. The word "we" appears often in it. The final sentence states, "And for the support of this Declaration, with a firm reliance on the protection of divine Providence, we mutually pledge to each other our Lives, our Fortunes and our sacred Honor."[1]

This lesson's Scripture is focused on building community. As you study, don't forget that your heritage and present experience in a community of faith came at a price. The Lord had a cross, our founders faced persecution, many veterans gave their lives, and others have made great sacrifices that have made possible our freedom to assemble in faith and fellowship with others.

In matters of faith, however, we could also affirm a *declaration of interdependence*. A favorite image of Paul is *the body of Christ*. That phrase recognizes our commonality as well as our individuality. We are dependent on God and on fellow believers. Whatever imagery we use to describe our common life together, we know that we are not flying solo through the universe.

2 Kings 7:3–9, 16

[3] Now there were four men with leprosy at the entrance of the city gate. They said to each other, "Why stay here until we die? [4] If we say, 'We'll go into the city'—the famine is there, and we will die. And if we stay here, we will die. So let's go over to the camp of the Arameans and surrender. If they spare us, we live; if they kill us, then we die."

[5] At dusk they got up and went to the camp of the Arameans. When they reached the edge of the camp, not a man was there, [6] for the Lord had caused the Arameans to hear the sound of chariots and horses and a great army, so that they said to one another, "Look, the king of Israel has hired the Hittite and Egyptian kings to attack us!" [7] So they got up and fled in the dusk and abandoned

their tents and their horses and donkeys. They left the camp as it was and ran for their lives.

⁸ The men who had leprosy reached the edge of the camp and entered one of the tents. They ate and drank, and carried away silver, gold and clothes, and went off and hid them. They returned and entered another tent and took some things from it and hid them also.

⁹ Then they said to each other, "We're not doing right. This is a day of good news and we are keeping it to ourselves. If we wait until daylight, punishment will overtake us. Let's go at once and report this to the royal palace."

. . . .

¹⁶ Then the people went out and plundered the camp of the Arameans. So a seah of flour sold for a shekel, and two seahs of barley sold for a shekel, as the LORD had said.

Nehemiah 2:17–18

¹⁷ Then I said to them, "You see the trouble we are in: Jerusalem lies in ruins, and its gates have been burned with fire. Come, let us rebuild the wall of Jerusalem, and we will no longer be in disgrace." ¹⁸ I also told them about the gracious hand of my God upon me and what the king had said to me.

They replied, "Let us start rebuilding." So they began this good work.

Nehemiah 4:6

So we rebuilt the wall till all of it reached half its height, for the people worked with all their heart.

Luke 10:25–37

²⁵ On one occasion an expert in the law stood up to test Jesus. "Teacher," he asked, "what must I do to inherit eternal life?"

> ²⁶ "What is written in the Law?" he replied. "How do you read it?"
> ²⁷ He answered: " 'Love the Lord your God with all your heart and with all your soul and with all your strength and with all your mind'; and, 'Love your neighbor as yourself.'"
> ²⁸ "You have answered correctly," Jesus replied. "Do this and you will live."
> ²⁹ But he wanted to justify himself, so he asked Jesus, "And who is my neighbor?"
> ³⁰ In reply Jesus said: "A man was going down from Jerusalem to Jericho, when he fell into the hands of robbers. They stripped him of his clothes, beat him and went away, leaving him half dead. ³¹ A priest happened to be going down the same road, and when he saw the man, he passed by on the other side. ³² So too, a Levite, when he came to the place and saw him, passed by on the other side. ³³ But a Samaritan, as he traveled, came where the man was; and when he saw him, he took pity on him. ³⁴ He went to him and bandaged his wounds, pouring on oil and wine. Then he put the man on his own donkey, took him to an inn and took care of him. ³⁵ The next day he took out two silver coins and gave them to the innkeeper. 'Look after him,' he said, 'and when I return, I will reimburse you for any extra expense you may have.'
> ³⁶ "Which of these three do you think was a neighbor to the man who fell into the hands of robbers?"
> ³⁷ The expert in the law replied, "The one who had mercy on him."
> Jesus told him, "Go and do likewise."

Hopeless People Become Helpful People (2 Kings 7:3–9, 16)

Elisha was the successor of Elijah as the prophet of Israel. His ministry spanned almost the last half of the ninth century before Christ. Those were bloody days. Life was hard in the Northern Kingdom where Samaria was the capital. Wars and rumors of wars were constant. During one time, the city of Samaria was effectively blockaded, and people were starving. Life indeed appeared hopeless, especially to four lepers who were huddled together at the city gate.

As the Scripture reveals, they saw no good alternatives. They could stay where they were, depending on a dwindling supply of handouts. They could go inside the city and die. Or, they could turn themselves over to the Arameans, camped outside the city. The worst that could happen was death, an end to their misery. Perhaps they could find something to eat and survive. Early in the morning, they left Samaria to put themselves at the mercy of the Arameans.

In the meantime, the Arameans heard some strange noises during the night. They thought they heard the sounds of an advancing army, with chariots and horses and many warriors. They had no way to verify these strange sounds of the night, and so they fled. When the lepers got to the Syrian camp, they found it empty of people but fully stocked with food

BAPTISTS AND FREEDOM

Baptists are freedom-loving people. History reveals that our founders treasured freedom. Although they shared many beliefs in common with other Christians, certain distinctive beliefs emerged from the early days in England and Europe:

- Religious freedom (freedom of, for, and from religion—no coercive power to enforce religion and no power to deny its free exercise)
- Soul freedom and the priesthood of the believer (the right and competency to relate to God without the interference of government, clergy, creeds, or other outside sources)
- Church freedom (the autonomy of the local church and the right to associate and cooperate with others as the local church chooses)
- Sometimes we misuse freedom and tear down community rather than build it. However, that does not diminish either the importance of freedom or the need to build community. As Paul wrote, "It is for freedom that Christ has set us free" (Galatians 5:1). Let us use our freedom responsibly, to build community.

and goods to plunder. So, they began to eat and drink, helping themselves to all that the Arameans had left.

A striking thing happened. In the midst of their good fortune, they realized "we're not doing right" (2 Kings 7:9). They realized that their people in Samaria were having a terrible time, frightened by the Arameans, hungry and thirsty, huddled together only expecting the worst. So, the lepers decided to share their good news with their fellow citizens of Samaria. They could have acted vengefully, thinking about how badly lepers were treated by their fellow citizens. They could have acted selfishly, keeping the bounty only to themselves. Instead they acted selflessly and lovingly. They went back to Samaria to share the good news and good fortune with their people.

The king was quickly told, but he did not accept the report at face value. He wanted it verified and sent messengers to do so. They saw the debris that had been scattered as the Arameans fled. Then the Samaritans left the city and plundered the enemy camp. Their food supplies were replenished, and people were able to buy and sell goods at a reasonable price.

The world of Elisha and the lepers was a difficult world. We could try to superimpose New Testament theology or twenty-first century thought onto their actions and beliefs. From this chapter in 2 Kings, we could debate the way lepers were treated, the ethic of war, plundering the goods of the enemy, and the death of a king's captain who had ridiculed Elisha and provided bad advice to the king. But none of this is the point

From a Child: A Plan for Community

When our grandson, Davis, became ten, our daughter-in-law baked a large chocolate chip cookie-cake and served it to him and his classmates at school. After all had eaten, some of the cookie-cake yet remained. One of the children came to her and asked, "Can you cut the rest of the cookie into smaller pieces so we all can have seconds?" Such a spirit from a fourth-grade child—willing to accept less so everyone could have some!

What can you share or even give up to make the experience of others better and the fellowship of your church stronger? Sacrificial and sharing people build community.

LESSON 5: *Building Community* 55

of the story for us today. In the context of the ancient world, where survival of the strongest often was the rule, we see the extraordinary action of the lepers. They knew it was not right to selfishly gorge themselves while their fellow citizens were in need.

"This is a day of good news," they said (2 Kings 7:9.) Good news must be shared. They appear also to have been stimulated by some healthy fear, thinking that if their story were found out, they might be punished for not sharing the good news with their own people.

In our time, we will probably not plunder an enemy campsite. We may not find a hidden treasure. But, we will have plenty of opportunity to share what we have for the good of the community. We all have gifts, both spiritual and material. When we share them for the good of the body of Christ, we build up the body as well as find satisfaction for ourselves. Along the way, if we also become more aware that "each of us will give an account of himself to God" (Romans 14:12), we will become a more responsible participant in God's good plans on earth.

Working Together (Nehemiah 2:17–18; 4:6)

Nehemiah lived in the fifth century B.C., about 450 years after Elisha and the four lepers. Many people had returned from Babylonian captivity and had been back in their homeland for almost a century. Some Jewish people were still away from their homeland, including Nehemiah, but they had a heart and interest in what was happening in their ancestral home. When word came to Nehemiah about the plight of people in Jerusalem, he was greatly troubled. He prayed. He began to feel led to try to do something.

Nehemiah was a ranking official in the king's court. As a cupbearer, he was more than a servant. He had significant influence on the king. He asked the king to let him return to his homeland and help rebuild the city. The king agreed, giving his blessing, protective custody in travel, and promise of supplies to help rebuild. Once Nehemiah arrived in Jerusalem, he kept his intentions secret. He made an inspection of the city walls and formulated a plan. Then he revealed that to key leaders.

When they heard the plan, they said, "Let us rebuild the wall" (Nehemiah 2:18). Although other nations around Jerusalem ridiculed Nehemiah's plan, even accusing him of secretly trying to overthrow the

Persian king, Nehemiah persisted and so did the people. They had specific assignments to do in their work, and they did them. Nehemiah 4:6 describes their success in a short time: they made significant work on the wall, for "the people worked with all their heart."

I once was pastor of a church that was located next to a river. Occasionally, the river and creeks flooded. Whenever that happened, the people came to the church building, ready to place sandbags, move furniture, and clean up the mess. Some great moments of fellowship came in the middle of the night, dealing with the water, mud, and muck. Gratefully, the people could also unite to do more than work on a building, for they were united in ministering to their community and being the people God wanted them to be. Working together builds community, and it also gives expression to the life we have in common.

The First Great Commission (Luke 10:25–37)

Jesus told the story of the Samaritan in response to a question from an expert in the Jewish law, "What must I do to inherit eternal life?" (Luke 10:25). Jesus turned the question back to him, asking him what he thought the law said about that. The man then essentially quoted what we call the *Great Commandments*: loving God and loving your neighbor as yourself. Jesus commended him for his answers.

Then the lawyer asked, "Who is my neighbor?" (10:29). The question revealed much about the lawyer and prompted a great story from Jesus. The expert in the law was looking for ways to limit his practice of love, thus revealing great need in his faith. Real love does not build fences; it opens doors. Real love does not seek limits; it seeks opportunities.

The Good Samaritan story is familiar reading. A man was traveling from Jerusalem to Jericho. Jesus' hearers would have immediately recognized that was a dangerous twenty-mile trip. The traveler was robbed, beaten, and left by the roadside. Two people, representative of groups designed to do good, looked at the beaten man. They chose to pass by on the other side of the road, ignoring a fellow human being in great need. Then a Samaritan came by. He gave first aid, took the man to an inn, and made provisions for his care until he could return. The Samaritan was an unlikely hero because he represented the most despised people Jesus' hearers knew. Modernizing the story, the pastor and the deacon ignored the person in need, but a _____ (fill in the blank with the person or group you most fear or dislike) became the hero of the story.

On telling the story, Jesus asked the man who he thought acted like a neighbor. The answer was obvious. The expert in the law got it right: "the one who had mercy on him" (10:37). To that, Jesus said, "Go and do likewise."

Most Bible students are familiar with a Scripture known as *The Great Commission*. That passage from Matthew 28:18–20 is a model for missionary-minded people. But, this passage from Luke 10 is also a *Great Commission*. God expects and commands Christians to have a merciful heart and to help people in need. Love is a command to act. We are not to be concerned with how little we can do to please God, but we are to be open to all opportunities to help fellow human beings. Loving God and loving neighbors are not either-or options. We are to do both, with forethought and with spontaneity, by intention and by chance.

Community Today

Churches develop reputations. Jesus said, "All men will know you are my disciples, if you love one another" (John 13:35). Is that part of your church's reputation? If it is, then an outsider might say, *That's a community I would like to be a part of.*

Our Scripture passages for this lesson have highlighted an unusual mixture of people: four lepers who did the right thing; a refugee who led down-trodden people to work together toward a common goal; and an outcast Samaritan who cared for a wounded man in great need. This mix of people may be looked upon as a strange assortment to reveal the will of God—but they do. If God can work through them in much more difficult circumstances than what we face, how much more could God work though people who profess to be united in our love for God and one another?

Almost every church has relational issues. I pray that we can relate more mercifully to one another in our church family. I pray that we also will reach out to other people who may not be just like us. Who are the lepers today, who are the downtrodden and displaced people, who are the Samaritans, who are the wounded in the ditch? Be a community builder, within the fellowship and in the world.

QUESTIONS

1. Why is *community*—genuine fellowship, a fellowship that works together—important to God and to us?

2. Consider the actions depicted in this lesson's Scripture passages—sharing with others, working for the common good, practicing genuine love, seeing and meeting needs, and being merciful to others. How can you and your class put such practices into action to build community?

3. When it comes to church, is the whole equal to or greater than the sum of its parts?

4. Who are the unreached and needy people who need a neighbor in your area?

5. In addition to your present ministries, what are some ways your church can connect and unite people?

NOTES

1. See http://www.archives.gov/exhibits/charters/declaration_transcript.html. Accessed 1/26/2010.

FOCAL TEXTS
Deuteronomy 10:17–19;
Matthew 25:34–40;
Luke 14:12–14; Hebrews 13:1–2

BACKGROUND
Deuteronomy 10:17–19;
Matthew 25:31–46;
Luke 14:1–14; Hebrews 13:1–2

MAIN IDEA
Because God has welcomed us and shown us hospitality, we are to welcome even people who are different from us.

QUESTION TO EXPLORE
Do we really have to show hospitality to and befriend people who are not our family, tribe, nation, kind?

STUDY AIM
To summarize the biblical teachings about showing hospitality and friendship to people who are different from me

QUICK READ
Our expression of hospitable love toward fellow believers, people who are different, and people who cannot reciprocate is a reflection of the grace God offers humanity though Christ's sacrifice.

LESSON SIX
Welcoming (Even) the Stranger

Genuine hospitality is wonderful. One summer a number of years ago, I served on a team that led revival services, sports camps, and evangelism training. Weekly, we moved to new churches, staying in members' homes to sleep, eat, do laundry, and sometimes, be entertained. We experienced different degrees of hospitality—some wonderful, some not so wonderful!

Two homes stand out in my memory. In the first, I felt genuine acceptance as I curled up on their couch swapping crazy family stories. Although our pasts differed, they welcomed and shared with me wholeheartedly. I still cook a recipe they gave me. Free to relax and be myself, I smile as I remember their openness and loving hearts.

The second home also brings a smile, but for very different reasons. It was a comedy of awkward silences and obvious inconveniences for the hosts. The experience culminated in a final supper during which my hostess described her intestinal issues and their accompanying surgeries. Not to be outdone, her husband detailed lancing his boils at home—all while we dined on spaghetti!

Thankfully, that was an extreme case for the summer, but I learned there's more to hospitality than mere friendliness. Throwing exciting, memorable parties, or privately entertaining family and friends with perfect place settings and polite conversation may all be elements of hospitality, but hospitality at its core is an other-centered attitude and a tremendous form of humility, because it focuses on the needs and desires of the guest, not the host. Such hospitality wants the guest to feel secure, peaceful, even complete. Hospitality means welcoming people for who they are, even if they are different. It means welcoming them because God welcomed us.

Deuteronomy 10:17–19

[17] For the Lord your God is God of gods and Lord of lords, the great God, mighty and awesome, who shows no partiality and accepts no bribes. [18] He defends the cause of the fatherless and the widow, and loves the alien, giving him food and clothing. [19] And you are to love those who are aliens, for you yourselves were aliens in Egypt.

MATTHEW 25:34–40

34 "Then the King will say to those on his right, 'Come, you who are blessed by my Father; take your inheritance, the kingdom prepared for you since the creation of the world. 35 For I was hungry and you gave me something to eat, I was thirsty and you gave me something to drink, I was a stranger and you invited me in, 36 I needed clothes and you clothed me, I was sick and you looked after me, I was in prison and you came to visit me.'

37 "Then the righteous will answer him, 'Lord, when did we see you hungry and feed you, or thirsty and give you something to drink? 38 When did we see you a stranger and invite you in, or needing clothes and clothe you? 39 When did we see you sick or in prison and go to visit you?'

40 "The King will reply, 'I tell you the truth, whatever you did for one of the least of these brothers of mine, you did for me.'

LUKE 14:12–14

12 Then Jesus said to his host, "When you give a luncheon or dinner, do not invite your friends, your brothers or relatives, or your rich neighbors; if you do, they may invite you back and so you will be repaid. 13 But when you give a banquet, invite the poor, the crippled, the lame, the blind, 14 and you will be blessed. Although they cannot repay you, you will be repaid at the resurrection of the righteous."

HEBREWS 13:1–2

1 Keep on loving each other as brothers. 2 Do not forget to entertain strangers, for by so doing some people have entertained angels without knowing it.

Let's Get This Party Started (Deuteronomy 10:17–19)

In the beginning, God graciously offered humankind every seed-bearing plant and fruit tree for their use (Genesis 1:28–30). Simply put, God knew their needs and provided to meet them, even without fine china. God's expectation for his people, then, was that they model his character and extend hospitality because of the grace they'd been shown.

This Book of Deuteronomy tells of God's covenant with the people of Israel. In verse 17 of Deuteronomy 10, God used his covenant name, *Yahweh* (LORD in English translations), which identified a contractual-type obligation for both parties. He followed it with "your" God, a definitive identifier of whose expectation was to be met. By clearly distinguishing himself, God communicated the solemnity of his calling to hospitality.

But the hospitality was not for God himself. Rather, God wanted it extended to the defenseless and the outcasts, those with no societal rights or who lacked a sense of belonging. In ancient times, as is often true today, a stranger attracts attention and is at risk of exploitation. The Hebrew word for "alien" (10:18–19) is *ger*, and the command to show hospitality to a *ger* occurs often. In fact, Leviticus 19:33–34 required that not only were aliens not to be mistreated, but they were to be treated as "native-born" and loved as oneself.

Hospitality is more than creating a feeling; sometimes it needs practical application. God instructed the people to show love by offering "food and clothing" (Deut. 10:18), and explained why: "for you yourselves were aliens in Egypt" (10:19). Human nature forgets too easily what it's like to be the outcast; God wanted the people to remember the isolation and vulnerability of that condition.

Just as hospitality was commanded in the Old Testament, Christ continued and expanded the requirement under his new covenant.

Party with a Purpose (Luke 14:12–14)

Occasionally, we throw parties *just because*, but we usually have an underlying purpose for hosting an event—a birthday, holiday, graduation, housewarming, or an expression of gratitude to a client. It might even be an *unbirthday* party like Alice attended in Wonderland! Jesus wants his disciples to party with a unique purpose in mind: to bless those who cannot reciprocate hospitality.

Invited to dine in the home of a member of the Sanhedrin, Jesus created a stir when he healed a dropsy victim (Luke 14:1–3). Eating with the Pharisee's family, friends, and rich neighbors, Jesus was presumably surrounded by the cream of Jewish society—people accustomed to honor and privilege. In fact, with Jewish protocol placing the most honored guests near the host, the guests selected the best seats at the table for themselves (14:7).

Observing this, Jesus made two bold statements. The first was to his fellow guests: "everyone who exalts himself will be humbled, and he who humbles himself will be exalted" (14:11). This kind of humility is the vulnerable attitude of Jesus and is a picture of the exaltation Christ will one day receive (see Philippians 2:5–11). Jesus' other bold statement, addressed to his host, was to encourage him to exalt the humble by welcoming the poor, crippled, lame, and blind into his home since they couldn't repay, knowing God would reward this choice (14:14). Jesus' call is away from public recognition (Matthew 6:1–6), and toward a countercultural life: loving, forgiving, and lending to those who don't deserve it (Luke 6:32–35).

Understand, however, Jesus is not opposed to inviting friends and family to celebrate life. The Gospels certainly picture Jesus dining with those he loved (see John 12:2, for example). But in contrast to the Pharisees, Jesus' hospitality earned him the label, "friend of tax collectors and 'sinners'" (Luke 7:34)! Believers frequently build walls or barriers on the basis of prejudices or differences, so hospitality is neither extended nor even desired with others (see small article, "Restrictions on Hospitality"). But Jesus sat down at the table with anyone, purposefully expressing the ever-reaching love of God. Whether praising a poor widow, welcoming children, healing the sick, or touching lepers, Jesus practiced unconventional hospitality, as we'll see by the King's guest list.

The Guest List (Matthew 25:34–40)

Seated on the Mount of Olives, Jesus' disciples came to him, asking questions about the end of the age (Matt. 24:3). In two chapters, Jesus revealed, largely in parabolic form, what to expect.

Matthew 25:31–33 pictures the separation of people as a shepherd divides sheep and goats: the sheep on the right, the goats on the left. And no, Jesus wasn't slighting goats! A sheep's wool made it more valuable than a goat, and thus Jesus chose sheep to represent those blessed by the Father and inheritors of his kingdom.

What actions did they take to indicate their participation in this inheritance prepared from the foundation of the world? They performed simple, basic acts of service (25:35–36) requiring no theological training, merely the power of hands motivated by hearts of love.

Food and drink meet humanity's most basic needs. Sheltering with clothing and a sense of community are next on the list of basic needs. Finally, visiting troubled, unproductive, socially shamed or unattractive people in their confinement reveals commitment to Christ. Each of these tasks addresses needs of the moment.

Verses 37–39 reflect the surprise of the sheep throughout the centuries. They can't understand how they directly ministered to Jesus. While certainly numerous individuals met Jesus' needs while he traveled Israel, those of us in the twenty-first century haven't had that personal opportunity. But Jesus says if we've ministered to even one person in these ways, we've ministered to *him*.

RESTRICTIONS ON HOSPITALITY

The basic Greek word for "hospitality" is *xenia*, from *xenos*, meaning *stranger*. Although most believers would like to exercise love for strangers (*xenophilia*), fear of strangers (*xenophobia*) is a reality.

Whether as an individual or a church family, it's difficult to exercise hospitality toward those we may view suspiciously. Instead of building bridges that nurture friendship and intimacy, we settle behind barriers of prejudice or grudges. The result is disconnection and estrangement, rendering us closed and inhospitable.[5]

Common rules and restrictions (inadvertently or intentionally) can lead us to welcome those like us and yet become barriers keeping out strangers. We have many subtle ways of making the unwanted feel unwelcome. The Christian community can, however, establish boundaries that differentiate it from the world while welcoming and caring for outsiders.[6]

Jesus' reply in verse 40 has been a matter of debate for Christians. Who are the "least of these brothers" of Christ? Theologians such as Luther and Calvin determined Jesus meant needy and persecuted Christians only.[1] Yet the majority view today is these "brothers" are any needy people in the world,[2] who, like Jesus, are "despised and rejected" (Isaiah 53:3). Therefore, Jesus' command to believers extends to all, for none are insignificant. In the assemblage of all heaven and earth, *everyone* in need qualifies to receive ministry—even angels!

That's Entertainment! (Hebrews 13:1–2)

In the first-century Mediterranean world, believers hosted in their homes itinerant preachers or those escaping persecution. Inns throughout the Roman Empire were places of questionable repute and danger for Christians. Even among non-believers, hospitality was a virtue and public duty, for mistreatment of strangers put the community's honor and religious security at risk. Among Greeks, strangers were under special protection from Zeus—patron god of guests—ready to avenge wrongs done to them. According to the myth *Baucis and Philemon*, Zeus assumed the disguise of a wayfarer and brought great blessing to those who indiscriminately treated him hospitably (see also Acts 14:11–12, where Paul and Barnabas are mistaken for Greek gods).

The New Testament letters reveal hospitality's importance in the unity of the early church (see 3 John; Romans 16:1–2; Titus 3:13; Philemon), and show what hospitality pragmatically involved: (1) exchanging letters of recommendation; (2) receiving guests into the household for a time; and (3) sending guests on their way provisioned.[3]

The Hebrews receiving this letter were certainly well-versed in Old Testament requirements to care for strangers, knowing they were to imitate Abraham's hospitality toward God's messengers (Gen. 18:1–16). These Hebrew Christians were now learning to emulate Christ's example of welcoming love. Jesus' command to his disciples was to "love one another" (John 13:34). Hebrews 13:1 reiterates the point of brotherly love (*philadelphia*, from *philos*, which means *love*, and *adelphos*, which means *brother*). Because hospitality is a fundamental expression of Christian faith, hospitality is to be shown to fellow believers, even if they are strangers.

> ## Case Study: An International College Student
>
> You've recently learned of a college student from another country who will have no place to go for the winter holidays. You know the student is a devoted follower of a different world religion, and you are sure he or she will be uncomfortable with your family's traditional, Christ-centered Christmas celebrations. Why or why would you not invite the student to stay with you? If you would extend the invitation, would you alter any of your traditions to help your guest feel more comfortable?

But love and hospitality involve risk. To help minimize that risk for the early church, *The Didache* (pronounced *Did-uh-kay*; a second-century handbook of Christian ethical instruction and church order) offered instruction for detecting imposters. For example, if visitors stayed more than two days or asked for money, they were to be considered false prophets.[4] Christians deceived by such imposters might be wary of offering hospitality again, but Hebrews 13:2 offers encouragement, noting that some who showed hospitality to strangers found they were entertaining angels. While we should not expect those whom we entertain to be supernatural beings traveling incognito, we can be assured that some of our visitors will prove to be messengers of God bringing words of blessing, instruction, or encouragement.

Meeting the needs of God's messengers through hospitality mirrors God's work with humanity. He knew humanity's deepest need was relationship with him, which could not come without forgiveness of sin. Our expression of hospitality to others is a response to the grace we've been shown, whether to those in the body of Christ or those outside it, whether like us or different.

Implications and Actions

Showing hospitality to others is an external expression of an internal attitude. God's expectation is not for us to meet every person's every need but rather to be sensitive to the value of human life with each opportunity. We are to recognize what that life can contribute to ours, taking care to avoid seeking personal advantage or domination over another.

You don't have to begin practicing hospitality by making a lifetime commitment of adoption. Try inviting a college student or widow(er) to share Sunday lunch, babysitting for a single parent or parents of young children, buying a cup of coffee for a stranger who appears discouraged, praying with someone in the hospital waiting room, or taking a gift to welcome a new neighbor. Perhaps you can help an evacuee from a natural disaster, become a foster parent, or host an exchange student. Crossing ethnic, socio-economic, political, or educational boundaries may be intimidating, even frightening. Remember, though, that as the early New Testament believers accepted strangers into their homes, bridges were built for creating unity in the body of Christ worldwide. Be creative, humble, and vulnerable as you identify needs and strive to meet them in the love of Christ.

QUESTIONS

1. What limits do you set on your willingness to show hospitality?

2. Where do you think Jesus was seated at the home of the Pharisee in Luke 14? Why?

3. Do you have difficulty being comfortable and welcoming to a particular economic, social, political, or racial group? Do you find barriers between yourself and people of other genders, physical/mental ability, educational background, or religion? How can you overcome the discomfort or barriers?

4. An indication that people feel welcomed in your presence is whether they linger, even when they should be going. Do people linger around you? Why or why not?

5. What are some advantages to showing hospitality to those who differ from us? disadvantages?

6. What are some attitudes and behaviors of someone you know who seems to exhibit biblical hospitality?

NOTES

1. Frederick Dale Bruner, *Matthew, A Commentary*, vol. 2 (Dallas: Word Publishing, 1990), 912.
2. Craig L. Blomberg, ed., "Matthew," *The New American Commentary* (Nashville: Broadman Press, 1992), 378.
3. S.C. Barton, "Hospitality," *Dictionary of the Later New Testament*, ed. Ralph P. Martin and Peter H. Davids (Downers Grove, Illinois: InterVarsity Press, 1997), 505–506.
4. *The Didache* 11:6–9. See www.earlychristianwritings.com/text/didache-lightfoot.html. Accessed 1/26/2010.
5. See Christian Reflection, "Toward a Welcoming Congregation," p. 10, from Center for Christian Ethics, Baylor University, at www.practicingourfaith.org/cfm/library/pdf/HospitalityStudyGuides.pdf. Accessed 1/26/2010.
6. See Christian Reflection, "Boundary and Hospitality," p. 12, from Center for Christian Ethics, Baylor University, at www.practicingourfaith.org/cfm/library/pdf/HospitalityStudyGuides.pdf. Accessed 1/26/2010.

LESSON SEVEN
Forgiving the Person Who Hurt You

FOCAL TEXTS
Matthew 6:12, 14–15; 18:21–35; Colossians 3:12–14

BACKGROUND
Matthew 6:7–15; 18:21–35; Colossians 3:12–14

MAIN IDEA
Because of God's forgiveness of us, we do not have the luxury of holding grudges and refusing to forgive.

QUESTION TO EXPLORE
How can we forgive someone who has wronged us?

STUDY AIM
To summarize New Testament teachings on forgiving others and to consider an occasion when I have forgiven someone or been forgiven by someone

QUICK READ
Jesus expects a high standard of believers when it comes to forgiveness of offenses. We must choose to mirror to others the depth of mercy God has shown us.

I'm not a *math person*. I have family members who are engineers and friends who teach math, but the joy for that subject matter is lost on me. Nevertheless, I manage to keep the checkbook balanced; I can figure out the area of a wall in order to buy paint; and I can help a ninth-grader with an algebra problem—usually.

What's nice about math is that numbers are concrete, unchanging. No matter the language or context, the functions of addition, subtraction, multiplication, and division aren't altered. So when Jesus talks with numbers in Scripture, I see the influence of Joseph's carpentry and laugh a little. I think God created math for the purpose of communicating his constancy. (Why else!) Thus, it's little surprise that on the matter of forgiveness, Jesus would use a constant, fixed, even rigid standard.

MATTHEW 6:12, 14–15

12 Forgive us our debts,
 as we also have forgiven our debtors.

. . . .

14 For if you forgive men when they sin against you, your heavenly Father will also forgive you. 15 But if you do not forgive men their sins, your Father will not forgive your sins.

MATTHEW 18:21–35

21 Then Peter came to Jesus and asked, "Lord, how many times shall I forgive my brother when he sins against me? Up to seven times?"

22 Jesus answered, "I tell you, not seven times, but seventy-seven times.

23 "Therefore, the kingdom of heaven is like a king who wanted to settle accounts with his servants. 24 As he began the settlement, a man who owed him ten thousand talents was brought to him. 25 Since he was not able to pay, the master ordered that he and his wife and his children and all that he had be sold to repay the debt.

26 "The servant fell on his knees before him. 'Be patient with me,' he begged, 'and I will pay back everything.' 27 The servant's master took pity on him, canceled the debt and let him go.

LESSON 7: *Forgiving the Person Who Hurt You* 71

> 28 "But when that servant went out, he found one of his fellow servants who owed him a hundred denarii. He grabbed him and began to choke him. 'Pay back what you owe me!' he demanded.
> 29 "His fellow servant fell to his knees and begged him, 'Be patient with me, and I will pay you back.'
> 30 "But he refused. Instead, he went off and had the man thrown into prison until he could pay the debt. 31 When the other servants saw what had happened, they were greatly distressed and went and told their master everything that had happened.
> 32 "Then the master called the servant in. 'You wicked servant,' he said, 'I canceled all that debt of yours because you begged me to. 33 Shouldn't you have had mercy on your fellow servant just as I had on you?' 34 In anger his master turned him over to the jailers to be tortured, until he should pay back all he owed.
> 35 "This is how my heavenly Father will treat each of you unless you forgive your brother from your heart."
>
> ## COLOSSIANS 3:12–14
>
> 12 Therefore, as God's chosen people, holy and dearly loved, clothe yourselves with compassion, kindness, humility, gentleness and patience. 13 Bear with each other and forgive whatever grievances you may have against one another. Forgive as the Lord forgave you. 14 And over all these virtues put on love, which binds them all together in perfect unity.

Reciprocal Forgiving (Matthew 6:12, 14–15)

When Jesus' disciples asked for instruction in prayer, he modeled for them adoration of God, supplication for needs, and petition for forgiveness. Although differences exist between the two versions of the Lord's Prayer (Matthew 6:9–13 and Luke 11:2–4), both include statements implying that *before* requesting God's forgiveness, the person praying will have already forgiven others.

Of all the elements of the Lord's Prayer, forgiveness is the only aspect on which Matthew showed Jesus elaborating, and it seems particularly harsh (Matt. 6:14–15). We aren't comfortable with the idea that our failure to forgive others will affect the well-being of our relationship with God. We want assurance that by humbly admitting our sin and requesting forgiveness, we gain restored fellowship with him (see small article, "'Forgiveness' and 'Debts'").

God is so passionate about unified relationships, though, that he not only forgives us but also demands interpersonal reconciliation among people. Our fellowship with others is damaged until we forgive those who sinned against us; then healing can begin. Failure to forgive on the interpersonal level means we can't be reconciled to God, and unity is broken.

Excusing or ignoring the offense is a misconception about forgiveness. Many people fear that forgiving the hurt or difficulty makes their experience and feelings void, to be glossed over or forgotten. C.S. Lewis said,

> There is all the difference in the world between forgiving and excusing. Forgiveness says, "Yes, you have done this thing, but I accept your apology; I will never hold it against you and everything between us two will be exactly as it was before." But excusing says, "I see that you couldn't help it or didn't mean it; you weren't really to blame." If one was not really to blame then there is nothing to forgive. In that sense forgiveness and excusing are almost opposites.[1]

Jesus asks us to forgive, not excuse or pretend the offender was nice when he or she wasn't. God never pretends to approve of our sin, either.

Another fear we have in forgiving is the offense will occur again. Therefore, many times it's easier to break contact with the offender to avoid exposure to repeated pain, but Jesus had something to say about that, too.

A Math Lesson (Matthew 18:21–35)

Peter seemed to have learned the lesson of Jesus' teaching in Matthew 6:12,14, 15 and 18:10–14. He apparently even desired to be a generously forgiving person, proposing to forgive fellow disciples seven times, a

LESSON 7: *Forgiving the Person Who Hurt You*

common biblical number for completeness that exceeded Jewish rabbis' requirement to forgive three times.[2]

But while Peter's question (Matthew 18:21) implied forgiveness should occur frequently, Peter expected there to be limitations. Jesus' stunning instruction (Matt. 18:22) is probably better translated "seventy-seven times" rather than "seventy times seven," but the point is clear. Rather than keeping track of the number of times we grant forgiveness, let forgiveness be an attitude, a state of mind. In what is probably intended to be a reversal of Lamech's law of revenge (see Genesis 4:24), Jesus took Peter's number of completeness and multiplied it, because his new covenant, the gospel, is a message of unlimited, divine forgiveness. Therefore, those who receive the forgiveness God offers should display their Father's character and show a forgiving attitude to others. If they don't? Jesus answered this question in the parable of the unforgiving servant (see small article "Expected to Forgive").

Unable to repay his enormous debt when called into account by the king (Matt. 18:23–25), the unforgiving (first) servant, his family, and their assets were to be sold in an effort to repay. Selling people into slavery to pay their debts was common in the ancient world, although in

"Forgiveness" and "Debts"

Forgiveness in the New Testament often is a translation of the Greek word *aphesis*, which has the basic idea of *release, let go, cancel, leave, set aside,* or *forsake.*

What are the "debts" forgiven? Jesus' word for "debts," *opheilemata* (Matt. 6:12; see 18:32) means *things due* or *deeds yet undone* (see also Romans 13:7). But in Matthew 6:14 and 15, Jesus' word for "sin," *paraptomata*, has to do with more specifically intentional or conscious acts of transgression.

All things considered, Jesus expects us to forgive others of the things they *haven't* done as well as the things they *have* done that offended us. This includes co-workers, family members, fellow believers, mere acquaintances, and complete strangers. We are not qualified or truly able to examine or evaluate the offender's motives. So, by repeatedly forgiving everyone we keep our personal accounts with God clear, too.

Judaism an Israelite could be sold for theft only under certain conditions (see Exodus 22:1–3; Leviticus 25:39–42).

In contrition, the first servant fell to his knees (Matt. 18:26), requesting not forgiveness, but patience. Astonishingly, the king pitied the servant and canceled his debt (18:27). Not only did the king not sell him into slavery, but he also did not require repayment or restitution of any kind! The servant asked for patience and a chance to repay, but he received much more than he asked: pardon—forgiveness.

Verses 28–30 reenacted the same scenario with different characters. The servant previously forgiven was indebted to by a fellow servant. The sum owed was miniscule in comparison to the previous sum, and yet the first servant choked his fellow servant and demanded repayment. Had he been going to prison for his debt, he might have had reason to demand the money due him. But he wasn't headed to prison; he was pardoned. The second servant pleaded for mercy, fell to his knees, confessed his debt, and begged for more time. Unlike the king, the unforgiving

EXPECTED TO FORGIVE

Found only in Matthew, Jesus told the parable in Matthew 18:23–35 in a style common for rabbis—a story involving a king with servants. The king usually stood for God; the servants, for God's people. Customarily, obedient servants reflected righteousness, disobedient servants represented wicked behavior, and settling accounts symbolized judgment.

The "talent" was the highest denomination of currency in the ancient Roman Empire, and 10,000 (*myrias*) was the highest number for which the Greek language had a particular word (root of the English word *myriad*).[5] Thus, the amount due the king was enormous, with estimates ranging up to one trillion dollars. For the first servant to promise repayment was prideful and unrealistic. But Jesus knew humanity sometimes makes vain promises to God. Yet like the king, God offers absolution.

Jesus wasn't teaching a doctrine of works for eternal security in this passage. He was focusing on the responsibilities of believers. He said in Matthew 5:7 that those who are merciful will receive mercy (see also James 2:13). So it is with forgiveness. People who would be recipients of forgiveness should expect to forgive.

LESSON 7: *Forgiving the Person Who Hurt You*

servant "refused" (literally *was not willing*)—a conscious, volitional denial of mercy—and chose instead to have the second servant thrown into prison.

Observing this, the other servants were distressed (18:31) and reported the situation to the king rather than taking matters into their own hands. Since the king's mercy was spurned, the king ordered the first servant to be imprisoned and tortured "until he should pay back all he owed" (18:32–34), a guaranteed life sentence.

Jesus' focus is on believers' responsibility to forgive. While this parable promises God's merciful forgiveness of our enormous debts, it also warns that forgiveness is impossible to the unforgiving and severe judgment awaits them. Our compassionate and merciful God cannot accept disciples who lack compassion and mercy, for it is the heart at which God looks (1 Samuel 16:7). Not only is it absurd for us to vengefully demand payment from others and refuse to grant forgiveness, but it also denies the only ground on which we stand before God—grace. To be unforgiving shows we misunderstand the principle of forgiveness.

Jesus, who lovingly took our deserved judgment on himself on the cross, said we would reveal our love for him by obeying his commands (John 14:15–24). His command is forgiveness. Forgiveness, therefore, is not regulated by arithmetic, but by Christ.

No Division (Colossians 3:12–14)

Jesus taught attitudes of gentleness, mercy, and peace (Matt. 5:3–9). Paul told the Ephesian believers to "be kind and compassionate to one another, forgiving each other, just as in Christ God forgave you" (Ephesians 4:32). Kindness, peace-making, and forgiveness are sometimes misunderstood as weakness, when in fact it takes more courage and strength of character to be forgiving than vengeful. Colossians 3:12–14 lists virtues expected of believers in social relationships within the church (see Galatians 5:22–23). They are opposites of behaviors found in Colossians 3:8. Just as God's kindness is intended to bring us to repentance (Rom. 2:4), God's children are urged to continue in his kindness for the purpose of reconciliation (see also Rom. 11:22).

In fellowship where true humility exists, there is freedom from tensions brought about by pride and personal agendas. Controlled, temperate

> ## WHEN FRIENDSHIP ENDS
>
> For a decade, friends Jack and Marty daily shared life over cups of coffee before work. They sat next to each other at football games and church. Their families regularly camped together and helped with household projects. Marty had emotional scars that affected his personality, and there were occasional disagreements, usually involving Jack's wife (Marty only tolerated her). Yet, everyone always forgave the offenses and moved on.
>
> But eventually, after all the years of friendship, Marty's sharp tongue, sarcasm, and unrealistic expectations finally wore on Jack, and he dissolved the friendship. Was Jack right? Why or why not? What should Jack have done? What would you have done?

reactions; patience; and forbearance—the willingness to put up with idiosyncrasies for the sake of fellowship—are strengths, not weaknesses as they are sometimes considered to be.[3] All of these must be volitional choices and actions, as we remember others endure us, too!

When Paul demanded forgiveness in verse 13, he used the verb *charizomai,* from the root *charis* (meaning *grace*), which means *to give freely or graciously as a favor.* Grace is imperative if we are to "bear with each other." Fellowship depends on our willingness to forgive, rather than to nurture grudges. We, though, are naturally inclined toward revenge, not reconciliation. Therefore, our motive for forgiveness is supernatural: "As the Lord forgave [us]."

As though echoing 1 Corinthians 13 and Romans 13:8–10, Paul stated again that love binds everything (and everyone) together in Christ (Col. 3:14). Christian maturity is best attained in a corporate experience (Ephesians 4:11–16; Hebrews 10:24–27). Pride breeds divisiveness, but when believers choose to direct their conduct with attitudes of peace, the family of faith will be united, not divided.

Implications and Actions

Humanity naturally focuses on other's offenses, nurturing grudges or planning revenge. As deeply as we desire justice for the offender, we

LESSON 7: *Forgiving the Person Who Hurt You*

desire God's grace for ourselves. Forgiveness is not fair; it is the outflow of mercy. Jesus calls us to show merciful forgiveness.

So, how can we forgive? Try these steps:

1. *Remember* God's mercy toward your own sin (Rom. 3:23; Eph. 2:3–5).
2. *Relinquish* your right to revenge. Let God settle the score (Rom.12:19).
3. *Release* the hurt. Repeatedly give it to God, if necessary. Every time you *rehearse* it, you make the pain deeper. But every time you *release* the hurt, the pain gets weaker.
4. *Refocus* on the hope of God's purpose for your life. What you focus on controls you. If you focus on pain, that's what you move toward. If you focus on hope and purpose, that's what you move toward (Job 11:13–16).
5. *Reach out.* Ask Christ to come into the situation and fill you with his love. Face the world; don't withdraw or put yourself in a shell. True love requires vulnerability.
6. *Respond* to the evil with good (Rom. 12:21). You don't overcome evil by criticizing it. You overcome it with good.[4]

QUESTIONS

1. How do you define *forgiveness*? Do you place limitations on the extent of your forgiveness? Are there extenuating circumstances in which limitations should exist?

2. In Jesus' parable, what do you think kept the first servant from seeing himself and his own debt in the pleas of the second servant?

3. Jesus doesn't tell us in his parable whether the second servant was released from prison by the king. What do you think? What ramifications can be drawn from the absence of this part of the story?

4. Doesn't even God's forgiveness have limits? Isn't that the meaning of the final Judgment? How is this reconciled with today's lesson?

5. Can you describe a time you forgave or were forgiven?

6. Take an honest look at yourself. Is there someone from whom you are withholding forgiveness? Is it possible you consider their offense to be worse than any you have committed against God or others?

NOTES

1. C.S. Lewis, "On Forgiveness," *The Weight of Glory* (New York: Macmillan Publishing Co., 1980), 122.
2. Craig L. Blomberg, "Matthew," *The New American Commentary* (Nashville: Broadman Press, 1992), 281.
3. R.E.O. White, "Colossians," *Broadman Bible Commentary*, vol. 11 (Nashville: Broadman Press, 1971), 247.
4. See "How To Forgive Someone Who Has Hurt You," *Purpose Driven Pastor*, Rick Warren, http://www.pastors.com/blogs/ministrytoolbox/archive/2009/08/20/how-to-forgive-someone-who-has-hurt-you.aspx. Accessed 1/21/2010.
5. Blomberg, 283.

FOCAL TEXTS
Luke 12:15–31;
1 Timothy 6:6–10, 17–19

BACKGROUND
Luke 12:13–34;
1 Timothy 6:2–10, 17–19;
Hebrews 13:5

MAIN IDEA
Christians living in a material world must put material things in the proper place in their relationship to God.

QUESTION TO EXPLORE
How do Christians in a money-centered society need to adjust their practices to Jesus' teachings?

STUDY AIM
To measure my approach to money and material things by biblical teachings

QUICK READ
According to the Bible, every disciple must work to put material things in their proper place in life. Material things can easily usurp the place of God.

LESSON EIGHT
Setting Right Priorities in a Money-Centered World

Just a few months after beginning my first full-time ministry position, my wife and I decided it was time for a new car. Hers was thirteen years old and was increasingly unreliable. The air conditioning was out. The car was pock-marked from a Waco hail storm. The paint was faded, the tires were bad, the windshield was cracked, and the battery was too big for the hood to close straight—giving it the appearance of sporting a lopsided grin. I spent about $250 getting it running so I could drive it to the dealership. There we received $200 for the trade-in.

Perhaps it was on the way home in our shiny new car that something profound happened to us. Our anxiety regarding the world unexpectedly skyrocketed. Are those bug splats on the front going to eat the paint? Is a hail storm forecast? We had better just stay home. We found ourselves parking a quarter-mile from the grocery store, lest a door ding or wind-driven shopping cart mar our new possession that we thought would give us peace of mind. We thought we had just bought a car, but in fact we had also just bought new worries.

Money and possessions have an incredible power in our lives. They promise so much in our culture: happiness, contentment, power, peace of mind, status, security. They deliver so much: worry, anxiety, covetousness, debt, relational discord, discontent. The Bible, and the Gospels in particular, make it clear that our handling of money and possessions is an integral expression of our discipleship.[1]

Luke 12:15–31

[15] Then He said to them, "Beware, and be on your guard against every form of greed; for not even when one has an abundance does his life consist of his possessions." [16] And He told them a parable, saying, "The land of a rich man was very productive. [17] "And he began reasoning to himself, saying, 'What shall I do, since I have no place to store my crops?' [18] "Then he said, 'This is what I will do: I will tear down my barns and build larger ones, and there I will store all my grain and my goods. [19] 'And I will say to my soul, "Soul, you have many goods laid up for many years to come; take your ease, eat, drink and be merry."' [20] "But God said to him, 'You fool! This very night your soul is required of you; and now who will own what you have prepared?' [21] "So is the man who stores up

LESSON 8: *Setting Right Priorities in a Money-Centered World*

treasure for himself, and is not rich toward God." ²² And He said to His disciples, "For this reason I say to you, do not worry about your life, as to what you will eat; nor for your body, as to what you will put on. ²³ "For life is more than food, and the body more than clothing. ²⁴ "Consider the ravens, for they neither sow nor reap; they have no storeroom nor barn, and yet God feeds them; how much more valuable you are than the birds! ²⁵ "And which of you by worrying can add a single hour to his life's span? ²⁶ "If then you cannot do even a very little thing, why do you worry about other matters? ²⁷ "Consider the lilies, how they grow: they neither toil nor spin; but I tell you, not even Solomon in all his glory clothed himself like one of these. ²⁸ "But if God so clothes the grass in the field, which is alive today and tomorrow is thrown into the furnace, how much more will He clothe you? You men of little faith! ²⁹ "And do not seek what you will eat and what you will drink, and do not keep worrying. ³⁰ "For all these things the nations of the world eagerly seek; but your Father knows that you need these things. ³¹ "But seek His kingdom, and these things will be added to you.

1 TIMOTHY 6:6–10, 17–19

⁶ But godliness actually is a means of great gain when accompanied by contentment. ⁷ For we have brought nothing into the world, so we cannot take anything out of it either. ⁸ If we have food and covering, with these we shall be content. ⁹ But those who want to get rich fall into temptation and a snare and many foolish and harmful desires which plunge men into ruin and destruction. ¹⁰ For the love of money is a root of all sorts of evil, and some by longing for it have wandered away from the faith and pierced themselves with many griefs.

· · · · · · · · · · · · · · · · ·

¹⁷ Instruct those who are rich in this present world not to be conceited or to fix their hope on the uncertainty of riches, but on God, who richly supplies us with all things to enjoy. ¹⁸ Instruct them to do good, to be rich in good works, to be generous and

> ready to share, ¹⁹ storing up for themselves the treasure of a good foundation for the future, so that they may take hold of that which is life indeed.

Investing in the Temporary (Luke 12:15–21)

Matters of money appear repeatedly in Luke's writings—the Gospel of Luke and the Book of Acts. Mary's song (Luke 1:46–55), Jesus' first sermon (4:18–19), the Beatitudes (6:20–26), the parable of the sower (8:5–15), the sending out of disciples (9:3–5; 10:2–12), the parable of the rich man and Lazarus (16:19–31), the rich young ruler (18:18–27), the parable of the minas (19:11–27), and the widow's gift (21:1–4) all address money and its proper place in the life of disciples. Acts describes the material sharing of the early Christian community (Acts 4:32–37), the danger of Ananias and Sapphira's exaggeration about giving (Acts 5:1–11), and the attempt by Simon to purchase the power of the Spirit (Acts 8:18–24).

Luke 12 provides some of Jesus' most direct words on the subject. Jesus was in the midst of his crucial journey to Jerusalem, and some of the most massive crowds yet had gathered around him (see Luke 12:1). In this chapter, Jesus' teaching was interrupted by a man wanting Jesus to mediate an inheritance dispute (surely the source of countless cases of family disintegration). In verse 14, Jesus attributed this attitude to greed and proceeded to tell a rather straightforward story.

A wealthy man had an excess of grain beyond his current storage capacity. Apparently the price of grain was lower than he desired, and so his goal was to store it for another day. This strikes us as a straightforward investment decision. Further, Jesus did not describe the man as corrupt in business practices or abusive of employees. As a result, the judgment in verse 20 on this man jars our modern, capitalist ears: "You fool!"

None of us wants such a judgment made on our lives. What was the man's error? The psalmist gave us the definition for this word: "The *fool* said in his heart, 'There is no God'" (Psalm 14:1, italics added for ...is). The man in this parable fit that definition. As is so often the ...ripture, the pronouns tell the story. This man's thought was dominated by *self*. The words "I," "me," and "my" appear repeatedly in Luke 15:17–19. In many ways this is a story that could have been taken from the headlines today. The rich man invested himself in his wealth and possessions, believing they bought security in life. Verse 21 reveals a dreadful poverty in his life—poverty toward God.

Ravens and Lilies (Luke 12:22–31)

Jesus used this occasion to instruct the disciples on matters of possessions and the worry they foster. We can understand the radical nature of Jesus' words in verses 22–23 if we remember that many people in that day were subsistence farmers. By definition, their worry was with the basics of life, including food and clothing. Jesus' disciples, to whom verses 22–23 were addressed specifically, were concerned about these basics, too. In this passage Jesus sought to lift the eyes and the spirits of his listeners from the burdens of the day and to see the reality of the kingdom of God.

Then, in verses 24–25, Jesus used two examples of a communication technique called *from the lesser to the greater*. If God cares for an unclean scavenger like the raven (see Leviticus 11:15), how much more will God care for us? Likewise, if God clothes the flowers of the field so beautifully, how much more will God do for us? Crucially, Jesus did not describe a life of flippant ease. Instead he described a life of striving—after God rather than after possessions.

In his years in the Soviet prison system, the *gulag*, Aleksandr Solzhenitsyn (1918–2008) experienced terror and suffering beyond belief. In addition to the horrors of the *gulag* staff's torture, thieves and thugs among the prisoners took a terrible toll. At one point in his account of his experiences, he described how gifts from family on the outside transformed prisoners into anxious cowards. As a result, Solzhenitsyn declared, "Own nothing! Possess nothing! Then no one will steal it from you, and you won't have to worry about it. And you'll be as free as a bird in heaven!"[2] Few (if any) of us could fully heed that advice. Too often, though, we slide without question into the consumer mode of our culture: striving for more, worrying more, and investing in the wrong things.

> ## THE RICH MAN IN FIRST-CENTURY CONTEXT
>
> The rich man in Jesus' parable would have seemed much more extreme and even exaggerated to the original audience than he does to a modern American. While he may merely strike us as a prudent businessman, Jesus' audience would have been made up of subsistence farmers. To hear of someone building barns for excess grain and for various other possessions would have been shocking—perhaps like today's stories of wealthy people building mansions for their pets or otherwise providing extravagantly for them.
>
> The rich man's decision also would have had greater community ramifications than we might initially recognize. His withholding of yields would affect the price of grain in the village, raising the cost of grain for everyone (Proverbs 11:26).
>
> In addition, his only consultation in the matter was with himself. The village culture in first-century Jewish life had a high degree of connectedness and webs of relationships. In this story, there is no steward or servant helping with management. We have a solitary person, making what would have seemed bizarre decisions, talking to himself. The label "fool" would have been perhaps less surprising to them than it is to us.[5]

Hazardous Material, Handle with Care (1 Timothy 6:6–10, 17–19)

Paul echoed Jesus' words on the topic in his letter to Timothy. In 1 Timothy 6, Paul was dealing with a key issue in the entire letter: false teachers sowing discord and confusion in the church. The element added in 6:5 to Paul's critique lies in their belief that "godliness is a means of gain" (1 Timothy 6:5). These opponents were trailblazing a tragic path, using religious influence for financial gain.

Like Jesus responding to the inheritance question, this instance of ⁱ sparked Paul's comments on money and wealth. In verse 6 Paul ir attitude and corrected it. Godliness plus contentment results ⁱn—just not the kind the false teachers were pursuing. This

LESSON 8: *Setting Right Priorities in a Money-Centered World*   85

is the gain of a well-ordered life like the one Jesus described in Luke 12:31. The proper attitude of disciples toward possessions is a contentment with having our basic needs met. Such an attitude is dramatically more difficult to achieve today than in the first century. Several other schools of thought from Paul's day (particularly the Stoic and Cynic philosophers) taught a similar message, praising the virtue of contentment. In contrast, we are bombarded with hundreds (some say thousands) of messages each day that are designed specifically to erode any possibility of contentment. Robert Frank, a professor of economics, described a phenomenon of competitive spending in our culture, not unlike an *arms race*, as we buy ever larger vehicles to feel safe, ever bigger houses to be near the right school, and ever more expensive clothing to make the right impression on others.[3]

In verses 9–10 Paul described the results of a covetous life. Whether rich or poor, a heart set on wealth sparks a downward spiral from temptation to harmful desires to ruin and destruction. This descent is not a passive force. Rather it is set as a snare and a trap. Unless we are on our guard and intentional about pursing a contented life, we risk this slide with its tragic end.

Certainly the most famous and most misquoted verse in this section comes in verse 10. If you conducted a *man on the street* quiz and asked whether the actual wording of verse 10 or the statement, *Money is the root of all evil*, was in Scripture, a great majority would probably pick the latter, *Money is the root of all evil*. Paul's comments are more nuanced than the blunt, popularized version. Paul said that it is the misplaced priorities of a heart set on money—"the love of money"—that is *a* source of "all sorts of evil" in life. The author of Hebrews made much the same point in Hebrews 13:5, "Make sure that your character is free from the love of money, being content with what you have." The love of money packs an idolatrous power to lead believers astray. Paul used the graphic image of falling on a sword. They have "pierced themselves with many griefs" (1 Tim. 6:10).

In verses 17–19, Paul continued on the general topic of wealth, correcting some potential misunderstandings. Some might conclude from his previous words that wealth in itself is sinful. Paul clarified that the place of wealth in our hearts makes the difference. Conceit in wealth and hope in possessions reveals a heart on the downward spiral of verses 9–10. For those in the congregation who had wealth, Paul prescribed a

> ## Ideas for Living with Contentment[6]
>
> - Don't be a passive consumer of advertising. Make a practice of making fun of the techniques marketers use to try to hook you.
> - Make room for generosity in your budget. Don't stretch yourself to a breaking point with purchases.
> - Buy things for usefulness rather than for the impression they'll make on others.
> - Take advantage of activities that are free.

life very different from one of complacent ease and indulgence in possessions. Rather, they are "to do good, to be rich in good works, to be generous and ready to share, storing up for themselves the treasure of a good foundation for the future" (1 Tim. 6:18–19). This is an eternal and imminently wise investment.

Long-Term Investments

Robert Harris ended his work of historical fiction, *Pompeii*, by describing the results of the tragic volcanic eruption that buried the city of Pompeii in 79 A.D.

> The ash hardened. More pumice fell. In their snug cavities the bodies rotted, and with them, as the centuries passed, the memory that there had even been a city on this spot. Pompeii became a town of perfectly shaped hollow citizens—huddled together or lonely, their clothes blown off or lifted over their heads, grasping hopelessly for their favorite possessions or clutching nothing—vacuums suspended in midair at the level of their roofs.[4]

Jesus and Paul agree that our handling of possessions has eternal consequences. If we were frozen in time, would future archaeologists find us clutching at possessions—or would they detect a different set of priorities?

This Lesson and Life

The New Testament's teaching on money is clear. The love of money crowds out God's place in our hearts and makes us captive to worry, obsession, and discontent. These passages give very practical advice for resisting the power and allure of a life dominated by things.

First, God must be in his proper place as Lord in our lives. We are to strive for obedience to God and to seek God's kingdom.

Second, we are to pursue contentment. While this is difficult in our culture, it is not impossible. Learn what erodes your sense of contentment. If window shopping sparks desires and discontent in your heart, find something else to do.

Third, practice generosity. One of the best ways to escape from the grip of possessions is to release your grip on them. Give to others. Share. Free yourself from a tyrant that wants to control your heart.

QUESTIONS

1. What possessions are the greatest temptation to you (clothing, cars, electronics, etc.)?

2. What causes discontent to grow in your heart?

3. What activities would help you to be "rich toward God" (Luke 12:21)?

4. What possessions cause the most worry for you?

5. Who else in the Bible had trouble because of greed, money, and possessions?

NOTES

1. Unless otherwise indicated, all Scripture quotations in lessons 8–9 are from the New American Standard Bible (1995).
2. Aleksandr I. Solzhenitsyn, *The Gulag Archipelago, 1918–1956: An Experiment in Literary Investigation*, Volume One (New York: Harper and Row Publishers, 1971), 516.
3. Robert Frank, *Luxury Fever* (Princeton, N.J.: Princeton University Press, 1999), 160.
4. Robert Harris, *Pompeii* (New York: Random House Publishing Group, 2003), 343.
5. Joel B. Green, *The Gospel of Luke*, The New International Commentary on the New Testament (Grand Rapids, Michigan: William B. Eerdmans, 1997), 489–491.
6. Richard Foster, *Freedom of Simplicity* (San Francisco: Harper & Row, 1981), 121–126.

LESSON NINE
Engaging in Honest and Just Business Practices

FOCAL TEXTS
Proverbs 11:1;
Micah 2:1–3; 6:8–15

BACKGROUND
Proverbs 11:1;
Micah 2:1–3; 6:6–16

MAIN IDEA
God calls for right living in how God's people deal with the business affairs of everyday life.

QUESTION TO EXPLORE
How does your Christian faith affect the way you engage in business affairs?

STUDY AIM
To decide on ways I will exercise my Christian faith in my business affairs

QUICK READ
A crucial part of living our faith is how we engage in business. God cares deeply about the honesty and integrity of our daily lives.

In our highly specialized and technological age, we regularly encounter situations in which we are at the mercy of the integrity of others. From the doctor to the plumber to the financial advisor, we essentially outsource important aspects of our lives—often without knowing the details. In many cases we can feel pretty helpless. When it comes to cars, I would not know a belt actuator from a flux capacitor, and so I am dependent on the honesty of those who know more.

One of the settings where I have felt this dependence quite keenly is in leading groups on mission trips. We land in another place, and one of the first stops is at the currency exchange. Depending on the location and the size of the team, I may need to change several thousand dollars. Reluctantly I slide the stack of dollars through the drawer, and back comes a much larger stack of worn, unfamiliar bills. Rarely is there time or security to sit and count it all right there, and generally I am still in a jet-lagged state. I feel essentially at the mercy of the person across the tinted glass.

Of course there is a flip side to these situations. Who is it that is dependent on your integrity? When do we feel the temptation to slip by with shoddy work and thus short-change customers, employers, employees, or coworkers? The Scriptures make clear that how we go about our work and engage in business each day is a crucial element of living out our faith.

Proverbs 11:1

A false balance is an abomination to the Lord,
But a just weight is His delight.

Micah 2:1–3

¹Woe to those who scheme iniquity,
Who work out evil on their beds!
When morning comes, they do it,
For it is in the power of their hands.
²They covet fields and then seize them,
And houses, and take them away.

They rob a man and his house,
A man and his inheritance.
³Therefore thus says the LORD,
"Behold, I am planning against this family a calamity
From which you cannot remove your necks;
And you will not walk haughtily,
For it will be an evil time.

MICAH 6:8–15

⁸He has told you, O man, what is good;
And what does the LORD require of you
But to do justice, to love kindness,
And to walk humbly with your God?
⁹The voice of the LORD will call to the city—
And it is sound wisdom to fear Your name:
"Hear, O tribe. Who has appointed its time?
¹⁰ "Is there yet a man in the wicked house,
Along with treasures of wickedness
And a short measure that is cursed?
¹¹ "Can I justify wicked scales
And a bag of deceptive weights?
¹² "For the rich men of the city are full of violence,
Her residents speak lies,
And their tongue is deceitful in their mouth.
¹³ "So also I will make you sick, striking you down,
Desolating you because of your sins.
¹⁴ "You will eat, but you will not be satisfied,
And your vileness will be in your midst.
You will try to remove for safekeeping,
But you will not preserve anything,
And what you do preserve I will give to the sword.
¹⁵ "You will sow but you will not reap.
You will tread the olive but will not anoint yourself with oil;
And the grapes, but you will not drink wine.

Business with Integrity: A Balancing Act (Proverbs 11:1)

When we think of "a false balance" and "a just weight," images relating to scales for weighing things, our minds may wander to the set at the doctor's office that always seems just a few pounds too heavy. In the Old Testament, however, scales were very important. They carried theological significance. Scales in their day would have been as common to commerce as cash registers or credit card readers are to ours. A product would be balanced against a set of weights or stones of standard measure. The possibility of manipulation came with subtle tweaks to the stones used for measurement. Deuteronomy 25:13–16 condemns the practice of keeping two sets of weights—one for buying and one for selling. We can detect the importance of this issue by how often it appears in Scripture. The passage in Deuteronomy just cited plus Leviticus 19:35–36; Proverbs 16:11; 20:10, 23; and Micah 6:11 all repeat warnings regarding the manipulation of scales.

In Proverbs 11, the sage minced no words in describing God's opinion of such practices. They are an "abomination" to the Lord. This same word is applied often in the Old Testament to describe idolatry (see 2 Chronicles 34:33; Jeremiah 16:18; Ezekiel 7:20; 16:36). Clearly God takes business integrity seriously.

While a few today might still face the temptations of a heavy finger on the grocery store scales, how else does this apply to our lives? In essence, this situation of "a false balance" may be invisible to the consumer. Perhaps it involves the computer technician whose wizardry and knowledge far exceed that of the user needing help. Or it could be the investment banker designing financial instruments far more complex than an outsider could grasp. It could be the sales representative, characterizing a product as new that has actually been reconditioned, or insisting that it is *guaranteed* to accomplish a certain task when there's considerable doubt it will or how long it will last. You likely can think of other possibilities.

Beware of any opportunity in your work that opens the possibility of taking advantage of others. In our hyper-competitive day, the difference between gaining an edge and taking advantage may appear to be a matter of perspective. God's word, however, is clear. A lack of integrity in business is "an abomination" to be condemned as severely as idolatry. On the other hand, honesty in business receives the high praise of God's "delight."

Power Corrupts (Micah 2:1–3)

Micah addressed some more brazen examples of corrupt business in chapter 2 of his prophecy for Jerusalem and Judah in the eighth century B.C. The opening word of the chapter is commonly translated as "woe." Another option is *alas*. This word was originally used in expressions of mourning at funerals (1 Kings 13:30).[1] With the subtlety of a single word the prophet pointed to the coming fate for those who practice corruption. With a heavy dose of irony, he was already mourning their loss.

Their character (or lack thereof) shines through in the second clause of verse 1: "Who work out evil on their beds." They lie awake figuring out how to cheat people, working out the next day's schemes for wealth and self-advancement. The people of Micah 2:1–2 had sold out to corruption and greed. The progression of verbs in this passage highlights the nature of their activities. They "covet," "seize," "take," and "rob."

Scripture provides a perfect example of this practice in 1 Kings 21. King Ahab coveted Naboth's vineyard, which was adjacent to his land. Naboth protested that this was his family inheritance. Queen Jezebel joined with Ahab in scheming to destroy Naboth and take the vineyard as their own. That's what they did. Their actions prompted a prophecy of doom from God through the prophet Elijah. Micah 2 is about the raw

The Meaning of Justice

"Justice" (*mishpat* in Hebrew) is a key word in Micah 6:8 and in Scripture as a whole. In modern usage, we tend to limit our thoughts about justice to matters of criminal justice and to people *getting what they deserve*. The biblical usage is much broader, however.

In addition to matters of punishment and judgment, *justice* alludes to the ideas of fairness, righteousness, and mercy in the light of God's work of salvation. Justice is described as a key component of God's nature and of what God desires in the world. The prophets, in denouncing the covenant unfaithfulness of the people, again and again called them to display *justice* in their dealings with the vulnerable as a way of demonstrating their right relationship with God. Amos famously declared, "But let justice roll down like waters And righteousness like an ever-flowing stream" (Amos 5:24).

exercise of power and about the judgment God will bring on those who abuse it.

Daily Sacrifices (Micah 6:8–15)

Micah 6 opens with a cosmic court scene with God bringing suit against faithless Israel. In verses 6–7, Israel responded with questions about what would make them right before God. What would fix it? What is it that God requires? Notice the escalation of ideas from burnt offerings, to prized calves, to massive offerings of rams and oil, to the suggestion of the firstborn—the most prized possession. In what may be the most well-known statement of Micah, God answered in verse 8. What God wants from us (a critical question for all humanity) is " . . . to do justice, to love kindness, And to walk humbly with your God." Israel suggested *Sunday* kind of activities to fix their relationship with God. God responded through Micah that it was *Monday through Friday* activities that he wanted to be made right. Paul echoed this idea in Romans 12 with that great opening challenge: "Therefore I urge you, brethren, by the mercies of God, to present your bodies a living and holy sacrifice, acceptable to God, which is your spiritual service of worship" (Romans 12:1). God desires faith lived in the day-to-day.

The imperatives of Micah 6:8 certainly have implications for business practices. "Justice" addresses the social relationships of life with commitment to one another, avoidance of oppressive or exploitative practices, and concern for the vulnerable. "Kindness" is a translation of the Hebrew word *hesed.* No one English word adequately bears its

---

APPLYING THIS LESSON

Pray for the wisdom and courage to live your faith with full integrity in your work.

Examine your heart and your work. Make sure that you have not justified laziness, shortcuts, or practices that shortchange or take advantage of others.

Choose a specific area of your daily life to improve, and take the extra steps to make it better.

meaning. In other passages we find translations such as *love, lovingkindness, covenant faithfulness,* or *covenant love.* This is *loyalty, kindness,* and *commitment* rolled into one word. The third element of God's desires, "walk humbly," denotes a life of priorities expressed before God. It presents a stark contrast to the scheming of Micah 2:1.

In verse 9, Micah shifted the image from a temple setting, with its question of what to present before God, to the heart of the city bustling with commerce. God's message makes clear he is not confined to the things of the temple. God cares about trade, business, and the working of the city. The rhetorical questions of verses 10 and 11 reiterate the importance of true measures, scales, and weights. Some scholars have suggested that verse 12 speaks of a legal setting. The "rich men of the city" were buying the loyalty of witnesses who would "speak lies" on their behalf.[2] The combined corruption of both commerce and the legal system led to the devastating picture of judgment in verses 13–16. God would frustrate their best efforts, making all their attempts at self-satisfaction—personal, family, business, investing, and agriculture—completely futile.

An Audience of One

Ponzi schemes, high finance deception, exploitative loans, executive bonuses amidst corporate meltdown, and credit card fraud have all littered the news over the last few months and years. These passages declare God's concern with this aspect of our world. This concern is not limited to the titans of Wall Street or the occupants of the executive suite. Every one of us must face the issue of living with integrity in our daily lives and work.

Will we be satisfied with half efforts or sloppy work? Will we justify even small acts of taking what is not ours with the idea that we are under-appreciated or that we *deserve* it? Will we comply with a policy or directive we know is not right or that we know is taking advantage of others? Will we exaggerate our hours, our résumés, or our roles?

We would do well to remember the words of Proverbs 11:1. How we do our work is judged by God as either an abomination or a delight. Paul's words in Colossians serve as an excellent guide. "Whatever you do, do your work heartily, as for the Lord rather than for men, knowing that from the Lord you will receive the reward of the inheritance. It is the Lord Christ whom you serve" (Colossians 3:23–24).

This Lesson and Life

While manipulation of scales and plans to seize land may seem like matters distant from our lives, the underlying issues of these texts have *direct* relevance to us. Some religious concepts, like deism, depict a God so distant from us that he certainly would not be concerned with the finer details of our lives. This is not the case with the God of the Bible. God cares about your work, your character, and your integrity.

These passages call us to resist the inner voice that whispers justifications for corners cut, for white lies, for helping ourselves, or for half efforts. The condemnation of false scales shows that God cares about the little things and about what we do when no one is looking. Integrity means that as we are to be honest and humble in our worship before God on Sundays, so we are to be honest and humble before God in how we do our work and conduct our lives the rest of the week.

QUESTIONS

1. What do you do when a supervisor or employer asks you to do something that may be unethical or harmful to others?

LESSON 9: *Engaging in Honest and Just Business Practices* 97

2. How have you seen people justify unethical or corrupt business practices?

3. What are the specific temptations in your field or line of work that would contradict Scripture's teaching?

4. How do you deal with a coworker who is engaged in unethical practices?

5. What are some ways you can "do justice," "love kindness," and "walk humbly" in your work and daily life?

NOTES

1. Leslie Allen, *The Books of Joel, Obadiah, Jonah and Micah* (Grand Rapids, MI: William B. Eerdmans, 1976), 286.
2. Allen, 378.

LESSON TEN
Exulting in the Marriage Relationship

FOCAL TEXTS
Genesis 2:18–25; Hebrews 13:4

BACKGROUND
Genesis 2:18–25; Hebrews 13:4

MAIN IDEA
God's provision is for husbands and wives to relate faithfully to each other in joyful intimacy.

QUESTION TO EXPLORE
How can the joy of the marriage relationship be maintained and enhanced?

STUDY AIM
To identify implications from the Scripture passages about how the joy of the marriage relationship can be maintained and enhanced

QUICK READ
The Bible reveals to us the original intent for marriage. It was intended to be a faithful and joyful relationship between a man and a woman for life.

The subject of marriage raises the emotional antennae of people more than any other subject. It does this for many people because they have experienced grief, disappointment, and betrayal in the marriage relationship. Maybe you are like the spouse who was asked whether she thought marriage was an institution. She answered, "You bet I do! It is like being in the penitentiary!" Obviously, she was not experiencing a joyful relationship.

Some who study this lesson will be uncomfortable because of the emotional baggage they carry from marriage. Some will be uncomfortable because they are not married but wish they were. For many people this topic is raw and painful.

On the other hand, many will react to this lesson with joy as they reflect on their experience in marriage. You and your mate are made for one another, and it is difficult for you to understand the struggles some people experience in marriage. It always touches my heart when I witness an elderly couple who have been married for many years still holding hands in public. I know more than one situation where one spouse sacrificially takes care of an infirm spouse as they struggle through their last days together but do so with love and joy.

What makes marriage a cause of either the heights of ecstasy or the depths of sorrow? The answers are legion. But the Bible does indicate God's intent for marriage. God intends that husbands and wives relate faithfully to each other in joyful intimacy.[1]

GENESIS 2:18–25

[18] The LORD God said, "It is not good for the man to be alone. I will make a helper suitable for him."

[19] Now the LORD God had formed out of the ground all the beasts of the field and all the birds of the air. He brought them to the man to see what he would name them; and whatever the man called each living creature, that was its name. [20] So the man gave names to all the livestock, the birds of the air and all the beasts of the field.

But for Adam no suitable helper was found. [21] So the LORD God caused the man to fall into a deep sleep; and while he was sleeping, he took one of the man's ribs and closed up the place with flesh. ²² Then the LORD God made a woman from the rib he had taken out of the man, and he brought her to the man.

²³ The man said,
"This is now bone of my bones
and flesh of my flesh;
she shall be called 'woman,'
for she was taken out of man."

²⁴ For this reason a man will leave his father and mother and be united to his wife, and they will become one flesh.

²⁵ The man and his wife were both naked, and they felt no shame.

HEBREWS 13:4

Marriage should be honored by all, and the marriage bed kept pure, for God will judge the adulterer and all the sexually immoral.

No Suitable Companion (Genesis 2:18–20)

Marriage was created by the Creator. In the beginning God created the heavens and the earth and when God looked upon creation he pronounced all things good. However, in verse 18 God pronounced something "not good." It was "not good" that the man God created should be alone.

Of course, both the Bible and experience indicate God gave some people the gift of singleness, and so this is no indictment of those who have chosen not to marry. After all, Jesus was single. So we can stipulate that singleness is not inherently bad.

But God did recognize that there needed to be a corresponding being to be a companion to the man, Adam. The word in verse 18 is translated in the NIV as "helper," and in the KJV as "help meet." In one sense, this is a rather unfortunate translation because in our culture a "helper" carries a connotation of a subordinate. However, there is no indication of subordination in this word. In Psalm 10:14 God is called a "*helper* of the fatherless" (italics added for emphasis). The word does not mean God is subordinate. Perhaps a better way to translate this word is *companion* or *one who corresponds with*. In other words, God knew Adam needed a new being who would be like the man, yet different.

Some people might argue the subordination of women based on Genesis 3:16. There God announced to the woman that her husband would "rule over" her. Note, though, that this pronouncement is made as a result of the introduction of sin into the marriage relationship. It was not intended to be that way from the beginning.

God brought the animals to Adam. It was clear from the moment the animals were created that they did not correspond to the man. The man, Adam, was given a role that indicated the animals were subordinate to the man. Adam was given the role of naming the animals. In Hebrew thinking, to name something meant that one had power and authority over it. Notice that Adam did not name his wife "Eve" until after the fall (Gen. 3:20). God gave animals to the man for the task of stewardship. The man was clearly superior to the animals. So in all of creation, there was still no being that corresponded with the man.

God Provides (Genesis 2:21–25)

God knew what to do. God knew just the kind of being the man needed to correspond with him. In beautiful imagery the biblical writer depicts God putting Adam to sleep and extracting a rib bone from his side. It is interesting that God formed Adam and the animals from the dust of the earth, but the woman was formed from Adam. The man and the woman were of one flesh to begin with, and they could be one flesh again in the marriage relationship.

Adam rejoiced when God presented the woman to him. He knew this gift from God was the perfect companion for him. It is difficult to see in written English, but the Hebrew text of verse 23 leaves no doubt as to the exuberant response of the man. Adam's statement in this verse is exultant and should have an exclamation mark after it! He immediately realized that this other human being was the gift God intended him to cherish.

I suppose it was easier in the days of Adam and Eve to recognize the spouse God intended each of them to have. After all, there were only two

LESSON 10: *Exulting in the Marriage Relationship*

of them! Of course, in our day the choices are considerably more numerous. However, I believe there is still a sense of exuberance when we find the right person. It has been so since the beginning.

The narrator provides commentary for us concerning the marriage relationship that speaks to every marriage in every time. It is what is called by some people the principle of *leaving and cleaving*.

First, marriage involves *leaving* the home in which one grew up. Adam and Eve did not face this situation since they did not have parents, but it does apply to every person since. If a person is not prepared to leave home, he or she is not prepared for marriage. Obviously, some cultures have social structures with extended families in the same household, or at least within close proximity. But the principle remains. There must be a sense in which a person recognizes the relationship they had with their parents has changed. The parental relationship is no longer the primary relationship a person has.

The failure of practicing this principle has been the ruin of many marriages. A spouse must make the marriage relationship primary, even above the relationship he or she has with a parent. Furthermore, parents must allow their children freedom to commit to the marriage relationship and relinquish their former roles. Doing this is difficult for some people, but the success of the marriage depends on it.

The second principle is that of *cleaving*. The word reminds us that a new social unit has been birthed that is separate from any previous social

GOD'S INTENTION FOR MARRIAGE

Jesus was asked about divorce in Matthew 19 and Mark 10. It seems to have been the same occasion. Divorce was a hot topic in Jesus' day because various Jewish factions had differing interpretations of the law concerning divorce. Some thought it was lawful for a man to divorce his wife for any reason whatsoever. Others thought it was lawful only in the case of adultery.

Jesus transcended the law and went back to God's original intention for marriage. He seemed to express weariness with the constant bickering over the law and pleaded for people to remember what God intended in the first place. Marriage is sacred. Marriage is permanent. Marriage is exclusive. It is not something to escape, but something to exalt.

relationships the spouse may have had. Uniting with one's spouse can be compared to a gardener's grafting one tree to another. (This illustration should not be pressed too far since marriage is a far richer experience, of course.) However, when trees are grafted the nourishment from one flows into the other, and the fibers from the other grow into the new partner. Soon, the two trees become one tree and produce fruit that is a mixture of both. They grow together so that to separate them does damage to both trees.

No wonder the death of a spouse or divorce from a spouse is so painful! It is like tearing apart grafted trees that have become one. When one person is left without the other, it does damage that is sometimes irreparable.

Genesis 2:24 pictures this relationship as becoming "one flesh." This picture is related to the sexual relationship that literally joins husband and wife. But there is more to a sexual relationship than simple animal instinct. It is a physical, emotional, and spiritual experience of two people that unites them.

Therefore, sexual relationships should be confined to marriage. Because the sexual act is emotional and spiritual as well as physical, it binds each person to the other in a unique way. Sex cannot be casual, regardless of modern cultural opinion.

Finally, the relationship between the first husband and wife was pure, at least until sin entered the picture in Genesis 3. They were "both naked, and they felt no shame" (Gen. 2:25). Shame did not enter the picture until sin entered the picture. In Paradise nothing had come between them. They had a perfect relationship with God and with each other. There was no guilt, and neither did they hide anything from each other. They lived in Paradise.

Case Study: Contemplating Divorce

A couple in your church is contemplating divorce. They have been to counseling, but nothing seems to help. How can your class help them? If they divorce, what could you and your class do to continue to minister to them?

Is Paradise Lost? (Hebrews 13:4)

Unfortunately, Paradise did not last forever. When sin entered the picture, God's original intent for marriage suffered a blow. That does not mean that we should not strive toward God's original intent, but it does recognize that marriage now presents challenges to many and failure to some.

The writer to the Hebrews offered a word of exhortation to the Christians in the early church. He reminded them that marriage should be honored because it was created by God. Also, he reminded them that God's intent was faithfulness in marriage.

Because marriage is a *one-flesh* relationship, adultery has no place in the Christian life. God grafted husband and wife together, and acts of adultery ruin what God has created. Adultery has disastrous implications for everyone. The adulterer is judged by God according to the Bible. But the damage goes beyond God's judgment. The betrayal of the one-flesh relationship causes damage and scars to one's spouse, not to mention the effects on children, extended family, and the church.

The marriage relationship should be one of faithfulness and joy. Strive to live in Paradise.

This Lesson and Life

How do you have a marriage that lasts for decades in faithful joy? It may sound simplistic in a fallen world like ours, but the short answer is: *Stay close to God, and stay close to each other.* When a husband and wife have a strong commitment to God and the will to strive toward God's intent for marriage, such commitment and effort go a long way in keeping the relationship strong. Sometimes a relationship does not survive, especially if one spouse—or both—have little or no intention of striving towards God's intention. But staying close to God does help us stay close to each other.

Thankfully, we live in the grace of Jesus Christ. Although failure in marriage is serious, whether it be the pain of divorce or the tragedy of adultery, Jesus gives us the opportunity to get back on track with God and with each other.

If you are happily married, praise the Lord! Serve as a positive example to others so they can learn from your success. But if your marriage is struggling or even failing, particularly if your spouse has failed you, remember that Jesus *can* mend broken hearts.

QUESTIONS

1. Genesis 3:7 states, "Then the eyes of both of them were opened, and they realized they were naked; so they sewed fig leaves together and made coverings for themselves." Contrast this verse with Genesis 2:25, "The man and his wife were both naked, and they felt no shame." What happened to their lack of shame? What are the implications of sin as it relates to marriage?

2. Do you agree or disagree with this statement by the writer: "If a person is not prepared to leave home, he or she is not prepared for marriage"?

3. Think about a couple in your church who have been happily married for fifty or so years. What makes their marriage successful?

NOTES

1. Unless otherwise indicated, all Scripture quotations in lessons 10–11 are from the New International Version.

LESSON ELEVEN
Helping Children Grow

FOCAL TEXTS
Psalm 128;
Matthew 19:13–15;
Ephesians 6:1–4

BACKGROUND
Psalm 128; Matthew 19:13–15;
Ephesians 5:25—6:4

MAIN IDEA
Children are a God-given treasure to be cared for and guided.

QUESTION TO EXPLORE
How can we best structure our lives, our homes, and our churches so children are cared for and guided?

STUDY AIM
To state implications from the Scripture passages about how children are to be cared for and guided

QUICK READ
A happy home understands the blessing of children and cares for them by establishing the foundation of the home on God.

From the moment a child is born, a parent's life changes forever. No longer can a husband and wife do whatever they want to do. Vacations are affected, finances are adjusted, and sleep patterns are destroyed, at least in the first few weeks. As children grow, the demands grow. School functions, sporting events, church activities, and a myriad of other things in life revolve around the life of this child.

For most people these adjustments are accepted as the cost of the welcomed blessing of having children. For some, however, the interruption of children causes resentment and impatience.

The Bible consistently welcomes the arrival of children as a blessing from God. In the ancient world, children were a sign of God's grace. Large families were a sign of wealth and blessing.

Today we do not necessarily equate large families with wealth and blessing. In our world, children are a financial liability rather than a financial asset. Unfortunately, some children are viewed as a curse to a family, and that attitude leads to abortion, abuse, and neglect. But the Bible reminds us that in every age children are to be valued as a gift from God and we have the responsibility of caring for them in our families, our churches, and our communities.

PSALM 128

1 Blessed are all who fear the LORD,
    who walk in his ways.
2 You will eat the fruit of your labor;
    blessings and prosperity will be yours.
3 Your wife will be like a fruitful vine
    within your house;
your sons will be like olive shoots
    around your table.
4 Thus is the man blessed
    who fears the LORD.
5 May the LORD bless you from Zion
    all the days of your life;
may you see the prosperity of Jerusalem,
6 and may you live to see your children's children.
Peace be upon Israel.

Matthew 19:13–15

¹³ Then little children were brought to Jesus for him to place his hands on them and pray for them. But the disciples rebuked those who brought them.
¹⁴ Jesus said, "Let the little children come to me, and do not hinder them, for the kingdom of heaven belongs to such as these."
¹⁵ When he had placed his hands on them, he went on from there.

Ephesians 6:1–4

¹ Children, obey your parents in the Lord, for this is right. ² "Honor your father and mother"—which is the first commandment with a promise— ³ "that it may go well with you and that you may enjoy long life on the earth."
⁴ Fathers, do not exasperate your children; instead, bring them up in the training and instruction of the Lord.

Build Your Home on a Firm Foundation (Psalm 128)

A happy home finds its foundation in God. While there are functional families that do not acknowledge God, families without the foundation of following the Lord will never be all they can be.

The psalm begins with a beatitude asserting that true blessedness comes from fearing God and obeying God's direction. The truly fulfilled family has God holding it up.

This does not mean that godly families will never have trial or sadness. Every family suffers from the maladies of living in this world. Grief, sickness, and financial distress can attack a godly family in the same way they attack ungodly families. But the family who follows the Lord has a strong foundation that can keep the home from crumbling.

Children need that kind of stability. They need to know that even in difficult times their family will continue to serve the Lord. The presence of the Lord provides security even when everything else is falling apart.

Many parents seem to have an innate understanding of the need for the Lord in their families. Often we get new families in our church who may have had no interest in godly things until their children were born. Countless times people have told me, *We want our children to come to church because we think it is important for them to have a spiritual foundation.* Adults who have not been in church for a long time, if ever, know that true blessings on their families can come only from having the Lord in their lives.

The psalm goes on to describe the family of the person who serves God. The psalm states that prosperity and blessedness will be measured by the number of children around the table. The wife is described as a "fruitful vine." This probably refers to childbearing. Like a grape vine produces fruit, so the wife produces children to gather around the dinner table.

We must be careful not to interpret these verses to mean that if a couple cannot or does not have children they have displeased God. We all know many godly couples who would like to have children but have never received that blessing. The psalmist is speaking in generalities, recognizing that children are a blessing from God. However, the lack of children does not necessarily mean we are in rebellion or cursed.

If God is the foundation of the home we will be blessed with or without children. When children do enter the home we recognize them as blessings from God who are to be cared for and guided.

The psalm concludes with the blessing of grandchildren. Someone has said that grandchildren are grander than children. The blessing of grandchildren is even greater when we have established the foundation of our home on the Lord. We are to leave a legacy of godliness to the generations that follow us.

Bring Them to Jesus (Matthew 19:13–15)

On one occasion little children were being brought to Jesus. Presumably parents had heard of the remarkable ministry of Jesus and were led by parental love to bring their children so Jesus could touch them and bless them.

The beautiful incident was marred by the disciples, who saw the imposition of children as a nuisance that interrupted Jesus' busy schedule.

LESSON 11: *Helping Children Grow*

Perhaps they were simply trying to protect Jesus, but their actions reflected an attitude that children were not very important.

Jesus did not share the attitude of the disciples concerning children. Jesus understood children as important to God's kingdom. Jesus knew that people entered the kingdom with childlike faith. Previously, in Matthew 18:5–6, Jesus had said, "And whoever welcomes a little child like this in my name welcomes me. But if anyone causes one of these little ones who believe in me to sin, it would be better for him to have a large millstone hung around his neck and to be drowned in the depths of the sea." Jesus was serious about caring for children.

Therefore, Jesus forbade the disciples to send the children away. The Gospel of Matthew says that Jesus "placed his hands on them" as a blessing (Matthew 19:15). The Gospel of Mark says that Jesus "took the children in his arms" (Mark 10:16).

Some people have used this text to validate infant baptism. There is nothing about baptism in this text and no indication that these children had faith. The parents were simply seeking Jesus' blessing, something Jesus was eager to do. While we cannot validate infant baptism from this text, we can know that Jesus valued these little ones as important in God's kingdom.

It is still the task of godly parents to bring their children to Jesus. While we cannot have faith for our children, we can teach them about God's grace and love and guide them on a path that leads them to Jesus. With parental guidance, children can understand what it means to express their own faith in due time.

How can families and churches bring children to Jesus? The best way is to begin pointing them in Jesus' direction from the moment they are born. At our church we have parent/child dedication services. This service is not baptism in any sense of the word, and the child does not

---

YOUR CHURCH'S MINISTRY TO CHILDREN

If you were talking to a family about attending your church and they said, *We are looking for a church that can provide ministries for our children*, what would you say? If you do not know what your church does to minister to children, research your church's ministry to children this week.

remember the event. But it is a time when parents dedicate themselves to raise their child in the arms of the church, where the child can be nurtured in spiritual matters.

It is important for children to be in church from the very beginning of life. As babies they begin to learn that church is a good and safe place to be. As toddlers they learn to trust adults and develop a concept of God. As children progress through the stages of Christian education they learn more and more about what it means to follow Jesus. One day, they will have a personal encounter with Jesus, and they will be able to express their own faith.

If you have a child who has not had the advantage of being nurtured in church from the beginning of life, now is the time to start regardless of the age of your child. It is never too late to bring children to Jesus.

Raise Them Right (Ephesians 6:1–4)

In Ephesians Paul wrote about the place of children in the context of a discussion about Christian home life. "Children, obey your parents" is one of the first Bible verses a child learns in Sunday School. Paul commanded obedience because it was right for the children. Obedience was for their well-being.

The exhortation to obedience was based on the Fifth Commandment, which Paul quoted: "Honor your father and your mother" (Exodus 20:12). Paul noted that this was the first commandment that was accompanied by a promise. The promise was connected to the Israelites living in the Promised Land. Does this promise mean that if we obey our parents we will live a long life as individuals? While it is true that obedience has kept many children alive by preventing them from doing foolish things, being an obedient child does not necessarily mean having a long life. On the other side, being a disobedient child does not necessarily mean having a short life. In the context of the Ten Commandments, a better interpretation is that God promised the Hebrew people that a society that honored and obeyed parents would be prosperous for many generations in the Promised Land.

This commandment reminds us that a successful society is a society that honors and obeys parents. Therefore, for the long-term stability of any society, parents must teach their children to obey.

LESSON 11: *Helping Children Grow*

Sometimes, in a desire to teach children, parents can make the mistake of exasperating their children. While the text speaks to fathers, it is no stretch of interpretation to apply this command to mothers as well. While it is important to teach children, we must do so with spiritual wisdom. Without patient spiritual wisdom, our efforts can produce children who resent the direction of parents. If a child resents the parents, the result will be the opposite of what God desires.

Implications and Actions

Raising children is a serious and difficult task. Children do not come with an instruction booklet when they are born. However, the Bible does help us.

Remember that a healthy family builds its home on the foundation of the Lord. This means parents must commit themselves to raise children to know God and to lead them to Jesus. These tasks do not need to be done alone. While parents are responsible for the religious education of a child, the church helps parents establish godly families by supplementing religious education and providing Christian fellowship. Wise parents bring their children to church so they can take advantage of every opportunity for building their home on the Lord.

Churches must be aware of the needs of families. The church must invest resources to provide quality experiences for the Christian education of children. Parents are looking for churches that provide for their children. It is the duty of the church to do all it can to help parents bring their children to Jesus.

QUESTIONS

1. What are some things your church does to minister to children? Can you think of other ways your church could minister to children and their families that you are not doing now?

2. Think about your parenting skills and experiences. Have there been times when you have needed to remind yourself not to exasperate your children?

3. How do you respond if your child is habitually disobedient? How do you think the church can help?

4. Why do you think the disciples tried to keep children away from Jesus? Have you ever had the attitude that the children in your church are not really important? How can you communicate to children in your church that they are important?

LESSON TWELVE
Being Sick and Getting Well

FOCAL TEXTS
Psalm 116;
Luke 4:38–40; James 5:13–16

BACKGROUND
Psalm 116; Luke 4:38–40;
2 Corinthians 12:1–10;
James 5:13–16

MAIN IDEA
We can trust God when
we pray for healing.

QUESTION TO EXPLORE
Can we trust God when
we pray for healing?

STUDY AIM
To summarize teachings from
the Scripture passages about
God's care when one is sick

QUICK READ
Illness offers opportunities
for Christians to witness
to a loving God. When we
seek God for healing, we
must also seek for God to be
glorified through our illness.

Monica was rushed to the hospital in the middle of the night for worsening flu-like symptoms. By morning, she was fighting for her life. That was three years ago. She has partially won that fight. She now lives a wholly different life than she lived before. Now Monica is a vent-dependent quadriplegic as a result of transverse myelitis, a neurological disorder.[1] She and her family have dedicated themselves to glorifying God through their circumstances.

Early in the process, when Monica was in the intensive care unit, she mouthed to her sister Leslie that she wanted a sign on her door. One had to listen very intently through her labored breathing to hear her whispered words. They were, "Please make a sign stating 'My God is an awesome God. For more information, inquire within.'" That sign alone witnessed to nurses, doctors, technicians, aides, volunteers, extended family, friends, and many more. Seldom a day passed without someone entering Monica's room to inquire about her awesome God. She and Leslie were happy to share! Leaving Monica's room without tears of gratitude to God was nearly impossible.

Is Monica well? In some ways, yes. In more ways, no. But Monica is trusting God every day for her daily existence as she, her family, and her friends continue to trust that God is able to heal either on this earth or in his eternal presence. Until then, God gives her breath. Praise God![2]

PSALM 116

1 I love the LORD, because he has heard
my voice and my supplications.
2 Because he inclined his ear to me,
therefore I will call on him as long as I live.
3 The snares of death encompassed me;
the pangs of Sheol laid hold on me;
I suffered distress and anguish.
4 Then I called on the name of the LORD:
"O LORD, I pray, save my life!"
5 Gracious is the LORD, and righteous;
our God is merciful.
6 The LORD protects the simple;
when I was brought low, he saved me.

⁷ Return, O my soul, to your rest,
   for the Lord has dealt bountifully with you.
⁸ For you have delivered my soul from death,
   my eyes from tears,
   my feet from stumbling.
⁹ I walk before the Lord
   in the land of the living.
¹⁰ I kept my faith, even when I said,
   "I am greatly afflicted";
¹¹ I said in my consternation,
   "Everyone is a liar."
¹² What shall I return to the Lord
   for all his bounty to me?
¹³ I will lift up the cup of salvation
   and call on the name of the Lord,
¹⁴ I will pay my vows to the Lord
   in the presence of all his people.
¹⁵ Precious in the sight of the Lord
   is the death of his faithful ones.
¹⁶ O Lord, I am your servant;
   I am your servant, the child of your serving girl.
   You have loosed my bonds.
¹⁷ I will offer to you a thanksgiving sacrifice
   and call on the name of the Lord.
¹⁸ I will pay my vows to the Lord
   in the presence of all his people,
¹⁹ in the courts of the house of the Lord,
   in your midst, O Jerusalem.
Praise the Lord!

LUKE 4:38–40

³⁸ After leaving the synagogue [Jesus] entered Simon's house. Now Simon's mother-in-law was suffering from a high fever, and they asked him about her. ³⁹ Then he stood over her and rebuked the fever, and it left her. Immediately she got up and began to serve them.

> ⁴⁰ As the sun was setting, all those who had any who were sick with various kinds of diseases brought them to him; and he laid his hands on each of them and cured them.
>
> ## James 5:13–16
>
> ¹³ Are any among you suffering? They should pray. Are any cheerful? They should sing songs of praise. ¹⁴ Are any among you sick? They should call for the elders of the church and have them pray over them, anointing them with oil in the name of the Lord. ¹⁵ The prayer of faith will save the sick, and the Lord will raise them up; and anyone who has committed sins will be forgiven. ¹⁶ Therefore confess your sins to one another, and pray for one another, so that you may be healed. The prayer of the righteous is powerful and effective.

The Grace of Deliverance (Psalm 116:1–9)

Before the psalmist even thought about telling the readers, or singers, about his problems, he was verbally jumping up and down with praise. God had heard his voice, and he was elated! When God heard the psalmist's voice, God also heard his supplications, or pleas. I love the phrase "he inclined his ear to me" in verse 2. Can you picture God leaning forward a little so he can better hear the whispers of a sick man?

The source of the circumstances from which the psalmist was delivered is not known for certain. Whatever it was, it was serious and threatened his life. Most scholars agree that his great affliction was a serious illness. He felt and believed that he was about to die. In fact, he was in such anguish that he compared his pain to "the pangs of Sheol" and declared he was encompassed by "the snares of death" (Psalm 116:3). This worshiper was sick and afraid!

What does "the pangs of Sheol" mean? The Hebrew teaching was that at death all people—both the righteous and the wicked—go to *Sheol* (Psalm 89:48). God had power over *Sheol* and was able to ransom souls from its depths (Ps. 30:3). This desolate place is compared to the farthest point from heaven (Amos 9:2). In the parallel structure of Hebrew poetry, *death* is often used in parallel with *Sheol*, meaning that *Sheol* refers to death (see Isaiah 28:15; Hosea 13:14).[3]

From his distress, anguish, fear, and desperation, the psalmist cried, "O LORD, I pray, save my life!" (Ps. 116:4). Such is the cry heard from many who are sick unto death. As a hospice chaplain I often ask a patient and/or the patient's family, "How do you want me to pray?" For some, their prayer is for God to save their lives. Others, accepting of their imminent death, pray for God's mercy, that God would come quickly and save them from the pain of this present life. The beauty of both of these desires is seen in the patient's turning to God for God's answer.

For the psalmist, God answered his prayer for deliverance. His soul could rest now, thanks to a gracious and merciful God. He could now claim "I walk before the LORD in the land of the living" (116:9).

Persistence in the Midst of Our Illness (Psalm 116:10–11)

Keeping our faith in the midst of illness is a challenge. For those who are daily walking the journey of illness while at the same time calling on the name of the Lord for healing, verse 10 should be a great encouragement. "I

ANOINTING WITH OIL

The Greek language has two words that apply to the customary use of oil in the ancient world, *aleipho* and *chrio*. When anointing was in a sense ceremonial, signifying God's special blessing, the word *chrio* was used (see Luke 4:18; Acts 4:27; 10:38; 2 Corinthians 1:21). The word *aleipho* was used more to describe pragmatic, therapeutic uses of oil, such as rubbing or massaging with it for medicinal purposes. James used *aleipho* in James 5:14, suggesting therapeutic anointing. This understanding of James 5:14 also indicates that praying does not substitute for practical and responsible medical treatment.

Olive oil was used often for medicinal purposes in ancient times. The specific kind of oil in this passage was olive oil, for that is the meaning of the Greek word used in James 5:14. The oil was applied to the body to provide help for various afflictions.[4]

kept my faith, even when I said, 'I am greatly afflicted'" (116:10). Keeping one's eyes on God is a must when those around you are not believing in healing. Possibly that was in the mind of the psalmist when he said, "I said in my consternation, 'Everyone is a liar'" (116:11). We must distinguish between the truth of God and the lies, or unbelief, of men and women.

For many years my daughter suffered excruciating migraines. They had come to the point of disabling her for days at a time. As a young mother of two, she struggled to care for her children on those days. A young woman in her church approached her one night after the worship service and said, "Laura, God has impressed on me that I am to lead in prayer tonight for your healing." This came as quite a surprise to Laura as well as to her friend. Healing was not one of the ministries offered in this church.

Gathering several young couples around Laura, her friend said to them, "If you can't or don't believe that God can heal Laura, please leave this group. We must be praying in total faith." No one left, and this wonderful group of young adults, inexperienced in healing prayer but obedient to God, laid hands on Laura and prayed for her healing. Laura did not have another debilitating migraine for more than three years. When these friends depended on the truth of God rather than their doubts, they witnessed a miracle and grew in their faith.

The Responsibility After Deliverance (Psalm 116:12–19)

The remainder of this psalm offers thanks for God's deliverance. Healing does not come without responsibility. This psalmist understood that concept and promised to pay his vows. He came to Jerusalem and offered a thanksgiving sacrifice in the presence of all God's people.

This Old Testament passage is a song of praise for God's deliverance. Recall the experience of Monica described at the beginning of this lesson.

> ## Case Study: Where Is God?
>
> Your close friend comes to you following her mother's funeral. She confesses to you that she is struggling with her faith. She had begged God to heal her mother, but her mother died. Now she is wondering whether there is a God at all and, if so, where was God when she needed him. How would you respond?

LESSON 12: *Being Sick and Getting Well*

Although Monica's deliverance from death has been answered for this time, she still struggles with her affliction. In the face of that struggle, however, she keeps her faith. Although Laura's healing was temporary, it was more than enough to increase her faith that God was more than able to deliver her from migraines. Neither of them has been permanently cured yet, but they have experienced healing. Both of these Christian women have received enough of an answer from God to pay their vows of thanksgiving in the midst of his people. Both are strong witnesses to the love of God wherever they go.

The Surprise and Anticipation of Healing (Luke 4:38–40)

The story of Simon Peter's mother-in-law's healing has long been a favorite of mine because I find such humor in it. Imagine staying home from church, or synagogue in this case, because you are sick with a high fever. You are perspiring and freezing at the same time. Your face is red, and you have an awful case of bed-head hair. Your eyes are tightly closed to shut out the light, and any noise whatsoever pounds in your head. Then your son-in-law brings the preacher home for lunch!

Simon and other disciples had just witnessed Jesus casting out demons on the Sabbath. Apparently from there they went to the synagogue. After services this unknown number of followers entered Simon's home. We do not know whether Simon already knew his mother-in-law was sick or discovered that when he came home. In either case, he was probably in trouble!

None of this mattered, however, when Jesus rebuked the fever. As the woman looked up from her sickbed, probably in disbelief that the guest preacher was staring down at her, she was at his mercy. There was no better place to be! When her fever left, she did as the psalmist in Psalm 116 did; she began to engage in service, in her case serving her guests.

This incident was early in the ministry of Jesus, and his reputation for healing was beginning to spread. In anticipation of healing, all those who had friends or family sick with various kinds of diseases came to him. Luke tells us, "and he laid his hands on each of them and cured them" (Luke 4:40b). Crowds began to follow Jesus, amazed at his miraculous deeds.

The Community of Healing (James 5:14–16)

Although James 5:14–16 is most often applied only to the healing of the sick, James emphasized praying together in faith. Even anointing with oil was secondary to prayer. Many scholars believe that since oil was commonly used for medicinal purposes, anointing with it was a confirmation that God also affirmed medical attention along with prayer.

What does healing look like in a community, or congregation, of believers today?

A beloved single mother of a five-year-old in our church had fought cancer for several years. Benita's cancer was in its last stages, and there seemed to be nothing else doctors could do. The pastor approached some of the deacons with the suggestion that our congregation come together for a healing service on her behalf. We invited a chaplain from a local hospital to lead the service. We first spent reflective moments in which we asked forgiveness of our sins, believing this to be an important part of preparing to pray for the sick.

Benita's mother stood beside her as the church gathered round her. People who felt led to do so were invited to put their finger on a small bit of compressed oil and apply it to her body. Prayers and tears were lifted to God in asking for healing of this precious servant.

Amazingly, healing of hearts and minds seemed to permeate the church body. More than physical healing was taking place in this service. Praying members lingered and began to pray for others in our congregation who were sick. Relationships were founded, and some were strengthened.

That was two years ago. Today, although Benita still lives with cancer in her body, she works full time at the church and is still enjoying life with her daughter. Our church still prays for her, and we still believe. God has been glorified.

Living Out Our Faith Today

Can God heal the sick? Obviously and absolutely! Then there is no better reason to approach God with humility and faith as we ask for healing for ourselves or a person we love. God is divinely capable. But we will miss God altogether if we seek only to be cured. Instead, as we invite God into

LESSON 12: *Being Sick and Getting Well*

our journey of sickness and ask God to be glorified, even with the ultimate hope of being cured we will experience healing in places we did not know we were sick. Healing will extend outward into our relationships and our church body. We will be changed. That in itself is healing.

Praying for healing is an exercise in learning to trust God. If we are expecting a quick fix, we must trust God because we likely will have to wait. In that waiting we will learn to trust God for who God is rather than what God does.

Putting our faith only in God's answer shortchanges us and God. When Paul asked that God remove the thorn in his flesh, God's answer was, "My grace is sufficient for you, for power is made perfect in weakness" (2 Corinthians 12:9). We can ask for no better answer.

QUESTIONS

1. What difference do you see in being cured and being healed?

2. How would you explain *deliverance* as used in Psalm 116? To what areas in our lives could *deliverance* be applied?

3. *All healing on earth is temporary.* Do you agree or disagree with that statement? Why?

4. Have you ever struggled with your faith because God did not seem to answer your prayer for healing? Was your faith strengthened or weakened?

5. As a church member, does James 5:14–16 give you comfort or make you uncomfortable? Why?

6. Think about someone you love who is ill. Can you see God's hand in the midst of the person's illness? Do you see *healing spots* in his or her journey? Where?

NOTES

1. "Transverse myelitis is a neurological disorder caused by inflammation across both sides of one level, or segment, of the spinal cord." See www.ninds.nih.gov/disorders/transversemyelitis/detail_transversemyelitis.htm. Accessed 1/27/2010.

2. Unless otherwise indicated, all Scripture quotations in lessons 12–13 are from the New Revised Standard Version.

3. Trent C. Butler, ed., *Holman Bible Dictionary*, (Nashville, TN: Holman Bible Publishers, 1991), 631, 1262.

4. A.T. Robertson, *Word Pictures in the New Testament*, vol. VI (Nashville, Tennessee: Broadman Press, 1933), 64–65; Charles R. Swindoll, *Jesus: The Greatest Life of All*. (Nashville: Thomas Nelson, 2008), 137; Joel C. Gregory, *James: Faith Works!* (Nashville, Tennessee: Convention Press, 1986), 115–116.

LESSON THIRTEEN
Relying On God's Care When We Face Loss

FOCAL TEXTS
John 11:17–26;
Romans 8:38–39;
1 Thessalonians 4:13–18

BACKGROUND
John 11:1–44; Romans 8:31–39;
1 Thessalonians 4:13–18

MAIN IDEA
When we face the reality of death, we can count on God's care and provision.

QUESTION TO EXPLORE
How can we access God's resources as we face the loss of a loved one—or our own death?

STUDY AIM
To consider how I have been able with God's help to deal with the loss of a loved one

QUICK READ
As believers we face death from a different viewpoint than does the world. Recognizing the transition is from this life to eternity with God, although hard at the time, eases the fear and dread of death.

The love story of British author C. S. Lewis and Joy Davidman was as poignant as it was brief. Although they married with the full knowledge that she was dying with cancer, they chose to live every moment to the fullest. Lewis was older when this marriage took place, and he had somewhat resigned himself to living alone the rest of his life. To love so deeply and then to lose the object of his love resulted in a spiral down into a grief he could not imagine. In his book *A Grief Observed* Lewis asks,

> Meanwhile, where is God? This is one of the most disquieting symptoms. When you are happy, so happy that you have no sense of needing Him, so happy that you are tempted to feel His claims upon you as an interruption, if you remember yourself and turn to Him with gratitude and praise, you will be—or so it feels—welcomed with open arms. But go to Him when your need is desperate, when all other help is vain, and what do you find? A door slammed in your face, and a sound of bolting and double bolting on the inside. After that, silence. You may as well turn away.[1]

Lewis's honesty with God opened up the door for truth. Often in our grief we believe to be Christian is to be stoic. Masking our grief through a put-on faith fools no one, though.

Our first passage for study begins with a friend's disappointment in Jesus. Martha's honesty opened the door for the greatest truth ever told.

JOHN 11:17–26

[17] When Jesus arrived, he found that Lazarus had already been in the tomb four days. [18] Now Bethany was near Jerusalem, some two miles away, [19] and many of the Jews had come to Martha and Mary to console them about their brother. [20] When Martha heard that Jesus was coming, she went and met him, while Mary stayed at home. [21] Martha said to Jesus, "Lord, if you had been here, my brother would not have died. [22] But even now I know that God will give you whatever you ask of him." [23] Jesus said to her, "Your brother will rise again." [24] Martha said to him, "I know that he will rise again in the resurrection on the last day." [25] Jesus said to her,

LESSON 13: *Relying On God's Care When We Face Loss*

"I am the resurrection and the life. Those who believe in me, even though they die, will live, 26 and everyone who lives and believes in me will never die. Do you believe this?"

ROMANS 8:38–39

38 For I am convinced that neither death, nor life, nor angels, nor rulers, nor things present, nor things to come, nor powers, 39 nor height, nor depth, nor anything else in all creation, will be able to separate us from the love of God in Christ Jesus our Lord.

1 THESSALONIANS 4:13–18

13 But we do not want you to be uninformed, brothers and sisters, about those who have died, so that you may not grieve as others do who have no hope. 14 For since we believe that Jesus died and rose again, even so, through Jesus, God will bring with him those who have died. 15 For this we declare to you by the word of the Lord, that we who are alive, who are left until the coming of the Lord, will by no means precede those who have died. 16 For the Lord himself, with a cry of command, with the archangel's call and with the sound of God's trumpet, will descend from heaven, and the dead in Christ will rise first. 17 Then we who are alive, who are left, will be caught up in the clouds together with them to meet the Lord in the air; and so we will be with the Lord forever. 18 Therefore encourage one another with these words.

Jesus' Power Over the Reality of Death (John 11:17–26)

"Lord, if you had been here..." (John 11:21a). I wonder how many forms of Martha's plea are raised to God on a daily basis today. *Lord, if you had stopped him from driving that fast. Lord, if you had kept her from becoming addicted. Lord, I begged you to keep him healthy for our family. Lord, if only....*

In spite of our *if onlies* the unthinkable has happened. We have lost someone we love. Even in long-term illnesses we have the tendency to continue to believe if only God would save them for a little while longer we would _____ (fill in your blank). Sometimes we can make preparations for the inevitable death. Other times we are caught completely off guard. In neither situation are we ready to let go.

Mary and Martha had a close relationship with Jesus, as did Lazarus. Although we are not told much about the friendship between Lazarus and Jesus, we read his sisters' impassioned plea for Jesus to come: "Lord, he whom you love is ill" (11:3). Their message implied they believed Jesus would come. He didn't.

This chapter in Scripture is one of the most tender of all stories told about Jesus. There is no doubt about Jesus' love for this family. The statements ". . . Jesus loved Martha and her sister and Lazarus" (11:5) and "Jesus began to weep" (11:35) afford us a look into Jesus' heart. However, Jesus also knew there was a greater miracle to come and a greater revelation of himself to be made. He intentionally stayed in Perea for two more days (see 10:40; 11:6).

First-Century Burial Practices

Burial practices in Palestine took place immediately after the death, usually within twenty-four hours. The dead were buried either in the ground or in caves or rock-cut tombs. Lazarus, obviously, was buried in the tomb. His arms and legs were bound with cloth, and his face was covered with a cloth (John 11:44).[2]

Because there was no way in the ancient world to monitor death or coma, most rabbis held theories about the impossibility of resuscitation after three or four days of death.[3] Some Jews believed the spirit hovered above a dead person's body for three days trying to get back in. On the fourth day the spirit left for good.[4] This may have been a factor in Jesus' decision to give time for this period to pass before he brought forth Lazarus.

Professional mourners were part of the funeral and mourning customs of that day (see Matthew 9:23; see also Jeremiah 9:17–18). The Jews sitting with Mary when Lazarus died, "consoling her" (John 11:31), may have been professional mourners.

LESSON 13: Relying On God's Care When We Face Loss

In an aside conversation with his disciples as Jesus began walking toward Judea, Jesus revealed he knew Lazarus had already died (11:11, 14). In fact, Jesus showed both great patience and a little frustration when he told the disciples Lazarus was asleep and they completely missed the point. Their minds were on the danger Jesus faced in returning to Judea. Although much of the time Jesus spoke in parables and questions, this time "Jesus told them plainly, 'Lazarus is dead'" (11:14).

Arriving after Lazarus died was not a slip-up on the part of Jesus. He was not surprised at what he found. Neither does God discover too late we have lost our loved one. The sisters had a great opportunity for trust at this point, and so do we. God hears our prayers and receives our message.

Turning to God in our grief, even if to blame God, is still an act of faith. We must believe God has the power to prevent our loss or it would be fruitless to approach God about it. Thus Martha's words of slight accusation were in keeping with her strong faith. They were also in keeping with her comfort to speak to Jesus in this way. Her relationship with Jesus was strong enough for her to express her disappointment. We can express to God our disappointment, too.

Martha immediately followed up with a statement of faith, "But even now I know that God will give you whatever you ask of him" (11:22). We cannot be certain whether she was asking Jesus to raise Lazarus from the dead. While it certainly appears that was her intent, the fact that she argued when Jesus actually started to open the grave would imply differently. Whatever her meaning, she still trusted Jesus even in the face of her great loss.

The conversation following Martha's greeting to Jesus provides a foundation of trust for all believers. "Your brother will rise again" (11:23) set the stage for Jesus to prove his deity to those gathered there. They witnessed a literal rising from the dead in front of their very eyes. Jesus revealed his power over death as Lazarus walked out of the tomb in his grave clothes.

But what about us today? "I am the resurrection and the life. Those who believe in me, even though they die, will live, and everyone who lives and believes in me will never die" (11:25–26). This beautiful, familiar Scripture promise reaches far beyond a miracle story in the Bible. Believers *today* can trust in a resurrection resulting in eternal life. The same question presented to Martha is offered to us in the face of our loss: "Do you believe this?" (11:26b).

Jesus' Power Through the Fear of Death (Romans 8:38–39)

Headlines in newspapers, television, radio, and the internet blare news of tragedies every day. We are surrounded by threats to life: natural disasters, car accidents, criminal attacks, war, and the list goes on. Calling out to Jesus in faith through a close personal relationship, as did Martha and Mary, seems to be the natural thing to do. But when we are traumatized through threats of death by unnatural means, where can we look in Scripture to let us know God is very present?

The entire chapter of Romans 8 is packed with promise of sufferings in this earthly body overcome by promise of a future glory. Paul did not skim over the fact that life hurts. But the passage reminds us it is life that comes against us, not God. When in this life we are most miserable, the Spirit bears witness with our spirit (Romans 8:16), and God is listening.

Paul asked seven questions in verses 31–35, all leading to one answer: *God is for us.* Perhaps the most quoted question is, "If God is for us, who is against us?" (Rom. 8:31b). Notice Paul didn't ask *what* is against us. *What* does not matter in the face of *Who*. Challenges such as "hardship, or distress, or persecution, or famine, or nakedness, or peril, or sword" are brought into submission to God.

Paul's question-and-answer quiz brought him to the conclusion that absolutely nothing could separate us from the love of God in Christ Jesus. First on his list of hazards was death. In nearly all versions of the top ten lists of things people fear today, death is included. However, even death and its earthly finality cannot separate us from the love of God. The list of items of dread and threat in verses 38–39, even though they may appear to be powerful, are no match for the love of God.

The bottom line of truth is actually the bottom line of verse 39: none of these things "will be able to separate us from the love of God in Christ Jesus our Lord." Nothing. If Jesus has power over death, then surely we can trust him to have power over our fear of death.

Jesus' Power Beyond the Hopelessness of Death (I Thessalonians 4:13–18)

In hospice the interdisciplinary team works together to help prepare families for the death of their loved one. Social workers rate the anticipated

LESSON 13: *Relying On God's Care When We Face Loss*

> ## CASE STUDY: A TRAGIC ACCIDENT
>
> A tragic accident takes the lives of two young people in your community. The family of one is a Christian family; the other family is not. One family appears to be grieving with hope, and the other, without hope.
>
> How do these two grief situations differ? How could the Christian family witness to the non-Christian family in the midst of their grief?

levels of grief, or bereavement, in terms of how much help will be needed. Low risk means although they grieve, their grief is normal. Moderate means there may be some complicating factors in their grief, such as several recent losses or the necessity of moving out of the home. High risk describes a grief that is likely to turn into violence toward oneself or another, or even cause thoughts of suicide.

The difference in low risk and high risk is measured by the difference in resources from which the bereaved can draw. Those at low risk have family, friends, and often a strong faith. Those in the high risk category have lost their hope. They have neither the support of family nor a faith strong enough to hold them up.

Paul also understood the difference between grieving with hope and grieving without it. Some Thessalonians had apparently expressed concern over the status of those who had already died. They were afraid if they were still alive at the time of Christ's return, they would go with Christ but those having preceded them in death would not. What would happen, they wanted to know, to their deceased loved ones?

In a beautiful declaration of Jesus' Second Coming, Paul assured his friends their loved ones would rise first at the sound of God's trumpet! Then those who are alive would be caught up in the clouds together with them. This kind of reunion comes only for those who are believers in Christ. In Christ is their only hope. Both the living and the dead are safe, and there is no reason to grieve hopelessly.

If hospice were rating these believers, the grief risk factor would be low. Would they be sad? Of course. Grieving? Certainly. But hopeless? Absolutely not!

Living Out Our Faith Today

There is an age-old adage that says, *Only two things in life are certain: death and taxes!* Actually, there are those who do not have to pay taxes. Death, however, happens on a ratio of 1:1. We will all die. And those we love will all die. These last two statements are monumental truths and have the capacity to overwhelm us with fear and dread.

As believers, however, we need not "grieve as others do who have no hope" (1 Thessalonians 4:13b). In fact, not only do we have the resources to carry us through the grief of loss, but we also have the responsibility to show the world a difference.

Trusting God even when God's answers do not seem timely takes faith. Trusting God when we are faced with overwhelming challenges to life requires courage. Trusting our deceased loved ones to God's care is difficult even for the best of Christians. In the end, however, if we have been faithful to believe, we can say with Paul: "'Death has been swallowed up in victory. Where, O death, is your victory? Where, O death, is your sting?' . . . But thanks be to God, who gives us the victory through our Lord Jesus Christ" (1 Corinthians 15:54b–55; 57).

QUESTIONS

1. Have you ever experienced the death of a loved one and found God to be seemingly absent? What was your experience?

LESSON 13: *Relying On God's Care When We Face Loss*

2. Have you ever bargained with God to save someone you love from death, but God allowed the loved one's death anyway? How did you respond to God?

3. What tribulations have come against you? How has God brought you through them?

4. If we should "not grieve as others do who have no hope" (1 Thess. 4:13), what should our grief look like? How can we mourn our losses as Christians?

NOTES

1. C. S. Lewis, *A Grief Observed* (San Francisco: HarperSanFrancisco, 1961), 1–2.
2. Trent C. Butler, ed., *Holman Bible Dictionary* (Nashville: Holman Bible Publishers, 1991), 215–216.
3. Walter A. Elwell, ed., *Evangelical Commentary on the Bible* (Grand Rapids: Baker Book House, 1989), 863.
4. Herschel Hobbs, *The Illustrated Life of Jesus* (Nashville: Holman Reference, 2000), 183.

Our Next New Study

(Available for use beginning September 2010)

THE LETTERS OF JAMES AND JOHN: *Real Faith*

THE BOOK OF JAMES: REAL FAITH IN ACTION

Lesson 1	Christian Living 101	James 1
Lesson 2	If You're Really Christian	James 2
Lesson 3	Words That Reveal Faith—or Not	James 3:1–12
Lesson 4	Want Peace? Start Here	James 3:13—4:12
Lesson 5	Living As If God Doesn't Matter	James 4:13—5:6
Lesson 6	Living Faith in Christian Community	James 5:7–20

THE LETTERS OF JOHN: TESTS OF GENUINE CHRISTIANITY

Lesson 7	Centering Life on the Word of Life	1 John 1:1—2:2
Lesson 8	Knowing We Know God	1 John 2:3–27
Lesson 9	Facing the Future with Confidence	1 John 2:28—3:10
Lesson 10	Loving to the Nth Degree	1 John 3:11–18; 4:7–12, 19–21
Lesson 11	Believing in God's Divine-Human Son	1 John 4:1–6, 13–16a
Lesson 12	Living By the Logic of Love and Faith	1 John 5
Lesson 13	Support God's Work Generously and Wisely	2 John 1–2, 7–11; 3 John 1–11

Additional Resources for Studying the Book of James[1]

> Joel Gregory. *James: Faith Works.* Nashville, Tennessee: Convention Press, 1986.
> Luke Timothy Johnson. "James." *The New Interpreter's Bible.* Volume XII. Nashville: Abingdon Press, 1998.
> Craig S. Keener. *IVP Bible Background Commentary: New Testament.* Downers Grove, Illinois: InterVarsity Press, 1993.
> Ralph P. Martin. *James.* Word Biblical Commentary. Volume 48. Dallas, Texas: Word Books, Publisher, 1988.
> A.T. Robertson. *Word Pictures in the New Testament.* Volume VI. Nashville, Tennessee: Broadman Press, 1933.
> Harold S. Songer. "James." *The Broadman Bible Commentary.* Volume 12. Nashville, Tennessee: Broadman Press, 1972.
> Foy Valentine. *Hebrews, James, 1 & 2 Peter.* Layman's Bible Book Commentary. Volume 23. Nashville, Tennessee: Broadman Press, 1981.
> Curtis Vaughan. *A Study Guide: James.* Grand Rapids, Michigan: Zondervan Publishing House, 1969.

Additional Resources for Studying 1, 2, 3 John

> C. Clifton Black. "The First, Second, and Third Letters of John." *New Interpreter's Bible.* Volume XII. Nashville: Abingdon Press, 1998.
> Raymond E. Brown. *The Epistles of John.* The Anchor Bible. Volume 30. Garden City, New York: Doubleday & Company, Inc., 1982.
> R. Alan Culpepper. *1 John, 2 John, 3 John.* Knox Preaching Guides. Atlanta: John Knox Press, 1985.
> William L. Hendricks. *The Letters of John.* Nashville, Tennessee: Convention Press, 1970.
> Craig S. Keener. *IVP Bible Background Commentary: New Testament.* Downers Grove, Illinois: InterVarsity Press, 1993.
> I. Howard Marshall. *The Epistles of John.* The New International Commentary on the New Testament. Grand Rapids, Michigan: William B. Eerdmans Publishing Company, 1978.
> Edward A. McDowell. "1-2-3 John." *The Broadman Bible Commentary.* Volume 12. Nashville: Broadman Press, 1972.
> Earl F. Palmer. *1, 2, 3 John, Revelation.* The Communicator's Commentary. Waco, Texas: Word Books, Publisher, 1982.
> A.T. Robertson. *Word Pictures in the New Testament.* Volume VI. Nashville, Tennessee: Broadman Press, 1933.

Additional Future Adult Bible Studies

The Gospel of John   For use beginning December 2010
Psalms: Worshiping the Living God   For use beginning March 2011

NOTES

1. Listing a book does not imply full agreement by the writers or BAPTISTWAY PRESS® with all of its comments.

How to Order More Bible Study Materials

It's easy! Just fill in the following information. For additional Bible study materials available both in print and online, see www.baptistwaypress.org, or get a complete order form of available print materials—including Spanish materials—by calling 1-866-249-1799 or e-mailing baptistway@bgct.org.

Title of item	Price	Quantity	Cost
This Issue:			
Living Faith in Daily Life—Study Guide (BWP001095)	$3.55		
Living Faith in Daily Life—Large Print Study Guide (BWP001096)	$3.95		
Living Faith in Daily Life—Teaching Guide (BWP001097)	$4.25		
Additional Issues Available:			
Growing Together in Christ—Study Guide (BWP001036)	$3.25		
Growing Together in Christ—Large Print Study Guide (BWP001037)	$3.55		
Growing Together in Christ—Teaching Guide (BWP001038)	$3.75		
Participating in God's Mission—Study Guide (BWP001077)	$3.55		
Participating in God's Mission—Large Print Study Guide (BWP001078)	$3.95		
Participating in God's Mission—Teaching Guide (BWP001079)	$3.95		
Genesis: People Relating to God—Study Guide (BWP001088)	$2.35		
Genesis: People Relating to God—Large Print Study Guide (BWP001089)	$2.75		
Genesis: People Relating to God—Teaching Guide (BWP001090)	$2.95		
Genesis 12—50: Family Matters—Study Guide (BWP000034)	$1.95		
Genesis 12—50: Family Matters—Teaching Guide (BWP000035)	$2.45		
Leviticus, Numbers, Deuteronomy—Study Guide (BWP000053)	$2.35		
Leviticus, Numbers, Deuteronomy—Large Print Study Guide (BWP000052)	$2.35		
Leviticus, Numbers, Deuteronomy—Teaching Guide (BWP000054)	$2.95		
1 and 2 Samuel—Study Guide (BWP000002)	$2.35		
1 and 2 Samuel—Large Print Study Guide (BWP000001)	$2.35		
1 and 2 Samuel—Teaching Guide (BWP000003)	$2.95		
1 and 2 Kings: Leaders and Followers—Study Guide (BWP001025)	$2.95		
1 and 2 Kings: Leaders and Followers Large Print Study Guide (BWP001026)	$3.15		
1 and 2 Kings: Leaders and Followers Teaching Guide (BWP001027)	$3.45		
Ezra, Haggai, Zechariah, Nehemiah, Malachi—Study Guide (BWP001071)	$3.25		
Ezra, Haggai, Zechariah, Nehemiah, Malachi—Large Print Study Guide (BWP001072)	$3.55		
Ezra, Haggai, Zechariah, Nehemiah, Malachi—Teaching Guide (BWP001073)	$3.75		
Job, Ecclesiastes, Habakkuk, Lamentations—Study Guide (BWP001016)	$2.75		
Job, Ecclesiastes, Habakkuk, Lamentations—Large Print Study Guide (BWP001017)	$2.85		
Job, Ecclesiastes, Habakkuk, Lamentations—Teaching Guide (BWP001018)	$3.25		
Psalms and Proverbs—Study Guide (BWP001000)	$2.75		
Psalms and Proverbs—Teaching Guide (BWP001002)	$3.25		
Matthew: Hope in the Resurrected Christ—Study Guide (BWP001066)	$3.25		
Matthew: Hope in the Resurrected Christ—Large Print Study Guide (BWP001067)	$3.55		
Matthew: Hope in the Resurrected Christ—Teaching Guide (BWP001068)	$3.75		
Mark: Jesus' Works and Words—Study Guide (BWP001022)	$2.95		
Mark: Jesus' Works and Words—Large Print Study Guide (BWP001023)	$3.15		
Mark:Jesus' Works and Words—Teaching Guide (BWP001024)	$3.45		
Jesus in the Gospel of Mark—Study Guide (BWP000066)	$1.95		
Jesus in the Gospel of Mark—Teaching Guide (BWP000067)	$2.45		
The Gospel of Luke—Study Guide (BWP001085)	$4.45		
The Gospel of Luke—Large Print Study Guide (BWP001086)	$4.85		
The Gospel of Luke—Teaching Guide (BWP001087)	$4.85		
Luke: Journeying to the Cross—Study Guide (BWP000057)	$2.35		
Luke: Journeying to the Cross—Large Print Study Guide (BWP000056)	$2.35		
Luke: Journeying to the Cross—Teaching Guide (BWP000058)	$2.95		
The Gospel of John: The Word Became Flesh—Study Guide (BWP001008)	$2.75		
The Gospel of John: The Word Became Flesh—Large Print Study Guide (BWP001009)	$2.85		
The Gospel of John: The Word Became Flesh—Teaching Guide (BWP001010)	$3.25		
Acts: Toward Being a Missional Church—Study Guide (BWP001013)	$2.75		
Acts: Toward Being a Missional Church—Large Print Study Guide (BWP001014)	$2.85		
Acts: Toward Being a Missional Church—Teaching Guide (BWP001015)	$3.25		
Romans: What God Is Up To—Study Guide (BWP001019)	$2.95		
Romans: What God Is Up To—Large Print Study Guide (BWP001020)	$3.15		
Romans: What God Is Up To—Teaching Guide (BWP001021)	$3.45		
Galatians and 1&2 Thessalonians—Study Guide (BWP001080)	$3.55		
Galatians and 1&2 Thessalonians—Large Print Study Guide (BWP001081)	$3.95		
Galatians and 1&2 Thessalonians—Teaching Guide (BWP001082)	$3.95		

Ephesians, Philippians, Colossians—Study Guide (BWP001060)	$3.25
Ephesians, Philippians, Colossians—Large Print Study Guide (BWP001061)	$3.55
Ephesians, Philippians, Colossians—Teaching Guide (BWP001062)	$3.75
1, 2 Timothy, Titus, Philemon—Study Guide (BWP000092)	$2.75
1, 2 Timothy, Titus, Philemon—Large Print Study Guide (BWP000091)	$2.85
1, 2 Timothy, Titus, Philemon—Teaching Guide (BWP000093)	$3.25
Revelation—Study Guide (BWP000084)	$2.35
Revelation—Large Print Study Guide (BWP000083)	$2.35
Revelation—Teaching Guide (BWP000085)	$2.95

Coming for use beginning September 2010

Letters of James and John—Study Guide (BWP001101)	$3.55
Letters of James and John—Large Print Study Guide (BWP001102)	$3.95
Letters of James and John—Teaching Guide (BWP001103)	$4.25

Standard (UPS/Mail) Shipping Charges*

Order Value	Shipping charge**	Order Value	Shipping charge**
$.01—$9.99	$6.50	$160.00—$199.99	$22.00
$10.00—$19.99	$8.00	$200.00—$249.99	$26.00
$20.00—$39.99	$9.00	$250.00—$299.99	$28.00
$40.00—$59.99	$10.00	$300.00—$349.99	$32.00
$60.00—$79.99	$11.00	$350.00—$399.99	$40.00
$80.00—$99.99	$12.00	$400.00—$499.99	$48.00
$100.00—$129.99	$14.00	$500.00—$599.99	$58.00
$130.00—$159.99	$18.00	$600.00—$799.99	$70.00**

Cost of items (Order value) _____

Shipping charges (see chart*) _____

TOTAL _____

*Plus, applicable taxes for individuals and other taxable entities (not churches) within Texas will be added. Please call 1-866-249-1799 if the exact amount is needed prior to ordering.

**For order values $800.00 and above, please call 1-866-249-1799 or check www.baptistwaypress.org

Please allow three weeks for standard delivery. For express shipping service: Call 1-866-249-1799 for information on additional charges.

YOUR NAME _____ PHONE _____

YOUR CHURCH _____ DATE ORDERED _____

SHIPPING ADDRESS _____

CITY _____ STATE _____ ZIP CODE _____

E-MAIL _____

MAIL this form with your check for the total amount to
BAPTISTWAY PRESS, Baptist General Convention of Texas,
333 North Washington, Dallas, TX 75246-1798
(Make checks to "Baptist Executive Board.")

OR, **FAX** your order anytime to: 214-828-5376, and we will bill you.

OR, **CALL** your order toll-free: 1-866-249-1799
(M-Th 8:30 a.m.-6:00 p.m.; Fri 8:30 a.m.-5:00 p.m. central time),
and we will bill you.

OR, **E-MAIL** your order to our internet e-mail address:
baptistway@texasbaptists.org, and we will bill you.

OR, **ORDER ONLINE** at www.baptistwaypress.org.

We look forward to receiving your order! Thank you!